So, You want to be a Coach...

So, You want to be a Coach...

The story of a Corporate Executive who became a Head Men's College Basketball Coach

Dr. Joe Brickner

Sunne Pharms Publishing
Shawnee, Kansas

ISBN 978-1-7354315-0-5
ISBN 978-1-7354315-1-2 (eBook)
Library of Congress Control Number: 2020915736

Library of Congress Publisher's Cataloging-in-Publication Data
Brickner, Joe, author.
    So, you want to be a coach : the story of a corporate executive who became a head men's college basketball coach / Dr. Joe Brickner.
    Shawnee, KS : Sunne Pharms Publishing, 2020.

    LCCN 2020915736 (print) | ISBN 978-1-7354315-0-5 (paperback) | ISBN 978-1-7354315-1-2 (ebook)

    LCSH: Businessmen--United States--Biography. | Basketball coaches--United States--Biography. | Basketball—Coaching. | Career changes. | Career development. | BISAC: BIOGRAPHY & AUTOBIOGRAPHY / Personal Memoirs. | BIOGRAPHY & AUTOBIOGRAPHY / Sports. | BIOGRAPHY & AUTOBIOGRAPHY / Business. | SPORTS & RECREATION / Coaching / Basketball.

    LCC GV884.C88 A3 2020 (print) | LCC GV884.C88 (ebook) | DDC 796.323/0924--dc23.

Website: www.drjoebrickner.com

Dedication

This book is dedicated to my wife, Connie, and my brother, Rocky.

Pursuing my "Dream Job" would not have been possible without the huge sacrifices made by my bride, both at the time the opportunity presented itself and then throughout the twelve years of being a coach's wife. She gave up career opportunities so that I could pursue mine. She provided unfailing moral support during the tough times. She continuously prayed for the success of the program and did whatever she could to help create that success. She still prays every day for the players and students that I taught.

My brother was the one who nurtured that competitive spirit that abides within me. Rocky was four years older than me, but was a constant companion growing up in rural Ohio. We competed at everything until he went to high school. I wouldn't trade those early years with him for anything.

Acknowledgements

I began to write this book in 2010, shortly after I was asked to resign from my head coaching job. I wrote a couple of chapters about my early years growing up, and felt comfortable writing about those times. I found, however, that when I started writing about my coaching tenure at Benedictine College in Atchison, Kansas, I wasn't in a place I liked being mentally. So I set the book aside and pursued other career opportunities, including being the CFO of a small drug development company. A few years later I picked up the book again, wrote a few chapters, but still did not feel "free" and comfortable documenting all the things that I experienced at BC. Finally, in 2019, nine years after I left the job, my mind was right to complete the work with what I feel is an honest, unemotional analysis of what I went through. I am glad I waited, for the fruits of my work at BC are now being witnessed in the lives of those who played in our basketball program.

There are many folks to thank for helping me sort things out and realistically analyze how effective I was as a coach and a mentor. My wife, Connie, is the first one to thank. She stood by me and assured me that the time I spent at BC was not wasted, and that there was so much more to what I did than just winning and losing games. Interestingly, she did not read any part of the book until I was done. At that point, she read the whole thing meticulously and made some critical observations, which I took to heart and used to make some revisions. I found that she remembered more things off the court than I did. She also made a suggestion that at first I was hesitant to do, because I was done and just wanted to finally go to press. Her suggestion was to add an Appendix containing comments from players today who had played for me 10 to 20 years ago. She thought their reflections on what take-aways each had from being in the program would say something about the positive or negative influence they experienced in our time together. Like usual, she was right. I have added an Appendix with former players' current comments, and I am so glad I did. It not only gave me an opportunity to reconnect with some of the guys I haven't talked to in a while, but it also allowed me the opportunity to hear what impact, if any, I had on these special people's lives. I hope you enjoy reading the Appendix as much as I enjoyed receiving the comments. As coaches or teachers you always wonder if you made a difference. After reading the Appendix, see what you think.

I'd also like to thank my good friend, Bill Toepfer, who gave me support similar to my wife. He also read the first complete draft, and, among other things, suggested I add a "Lesson" at the end of each Chapter. He thought it would be a good tool for men and women who want to be coaches to be able to help guide them in pursuit of their dream.

Mike Tharp, a former college teammate and an extremely successful journalist for some of the most prestigious media giants in the world, edited the book for me. His guidance was critical, as is his friendship. Having worked all over the world (as well as having played basketball too), his perspective was much wider than mine. His contributions were so valuable.

My son, Scott, really helped with suggestions for the business vs. sports perspective, as did his brother, Alex. A college classmate, Bob Settich, gave me valuable advice on self-publishing. John Brown, a former NBA player and later an AAU teammate and good friend of mine, was gracious enough to write the Forward. Terry Hanson, a former Ted Turner executive, also reviewed the book and contributed his opinion on the back cover.

I want to thank Benedictine College and St. Benedict's Abbey for allowing me to use a number of photos from various college and abbey publications. There sure are good people up on that hill!

I would also like to acknowledge the players. They were good kids who turned into good men. Most of them played hard for me and bought into the system. I wish I could have led them to the national tournament – we were so close a couple of times – but that was not in the cards. I hope that I still made the experience one they wouldn't trade for anything.

Finally, I want to thank God. He has been so good to me for 70+ years. He always made sure we had enough to cover the necessities, and he put people in my pathway that had such a positive influence on me. He's been there when I have been down, and He has been there when I've been up. He has allowed me to have a wonderful spiritual life and blessed me with a wonderful family. I guess my mom must have prayed really hard for me!

Table of Contents

Detailed Table of Contents

Exhibits

Forward

I have known Joe for over 30 years and I consider him one of the most honorable men I have known. It was pure joy getting to play senior basketball with Joe. We were able to win multiple championships together on a national stage and to a large part, it was because of Joe. Not only was he a great player, but he coached our teams. Ultimately, I think his number one asset is toughness, both mentally and physically. There was never any quit in Joe.

When most people think of coaching college basketball, they think of John Calipari at Kentucky or (if you're a little older) John Wooden at UCLA and his amazing run. This book takes you into a world most do not understand, coaching at a small school with limited finances. Joe is brutally honest on his challenges of trying to upgrade facilities and obtaining more scholarship money. He also explains how his time with Southwestern Bell in the business world helped him garner the resources to achieve many of his goals.

This book is a must read for anyone contemplating coaching. Joe does not gloss over the mental and financial challenges of coaching at a small school. But what you will see in this book is an unbelievable love and respect for the game of basketball and the many lives he touched.

John Brown
Mizzou All-American
First-round Draft Choice & Multiple Year Starter for the Atlanta Hawks

Introduction

"Dreams are extremely important. You can't do it unless you imagine it." (George Lucas, American Filmmaker)

I n my past life in Corporate America, as well as in my informal discussions with friends and acquaintances, the question often came up "If money wasn't a factor and you could do anything you wanted to do, what would it be?" More often than not the response was "I'd like to be a coach." It didn't matter if I was talking to a vice-president or a janitor, the answer was the same. It seems like people always want to be sports coaches. Well, after nearly 28 years making a living in Corporate America, I actually got the opportunity to be a coach – a full-fledged college men's head basketball coach!

This book is a look at the ups and downs of coaching, what parallels there are between coaching and managing groups of people in a business setting, and why I believe folks think that being a coach is their "Dream Job."

- If you have ever wondered what it is like behind the scenes of coaching at the college level, this book will give you actual examples of the daily life of a college basketball coach. You will share the highs and the lows of coaching; the happy days and the not-so-happy days; the enjoyable tasks and the not-so-enjoyable tasks.
- If you have ever wondered if the parallels of business management and sports coaching are as pervasive as some folks think they are, this book will compare the actual experiences of performing both jobs.
- If you have ever wondered why so many people want to be coaches, this book will share some insight into the altruism that just may drive that desire.

Background

The Early Years

"We are not only our brother's keeper; in countless large and small ways, we are our brother's maker." (Bonaro Overstreet, American poet and psychologist)

Mom and 3 of 4 kids

I grew up in a small industrial town in northwestern Ohio, one of four children of a somewhat poor family. (One Christmas I got a Canadian Club tie clip – I didn't own a tie – and my brother got a Citizens Bank money clip – he had no money.) My father sold automobiles (not many) and my mom worked at a Westinghouse factory winding jet motors on an assembly line until my sister was born – then she stayed home with us kids. We lived paycheck to paycheck, like many in that community. The people in that part of Ohio were either farmers or worked in the local factories. We were a typical Catholic family – two boys, two girls, attended the local Catholic schools, and lived with Grandma and Grandpa on the farm for a while until mom and dad could afford to rent a neighboring farmhouse. As all Ohio boys did, you first finished your chores and then you went out and played ball until supper. The ball you played depended upon the season. Back then we were only aware of three sports: football, basketball, and baseball. We played football in the neighbor's front yard, basketball in the barn, and baseball in the pasture where the cows grazed. (Fortunately, we Ohio boys are smart enough not to play football in the cow pasture!)

My favorite sport was basketball, either because I didn't like wiping cow manure off of the baseball all the time or because I was better at basketball than the other two sports. I was lucky enough to have a brother who was only a little bit bigger than me, even though he was four years older. His name was Don, but everyone at school called him "Rocky." (Obviously from our last name - BRICKner. Those Ohio kids have always been one step ahead of the rest of the country.) My brother is probably most responsible for my competitive nature. We competed against each other in everything. If we were inside, we'd play cards (he'd win), checkers (I'd win), or monopoly (we'd fight). If we were outside and not playing ball, we'd race our bikes around the oval driveway in front of Grandpa's barn. This also ended badly – at least for me.

I'd be Indy 500's Billy Vukovich, he'd be the local Allentown Speedway's Don Lawnbrake, and we'd go for 100 laps. Inevitably somewhere between the 95th and the 99th lap, Rocky would make sure I was on the outside lane as we came around the curve heading down the backstretch. He would crowd me over until I hit the barn and got wiped out, and he'd win. (Fortunately, we wore our race-car helmets, for this was pre-dating the ubiquitous use of the bicycle helmets worn today.) Don't feel too sorry for me, though, for I always seemed to even things up, even if it was accidently. For example, one July 4th he needed quite a few stitches after walking in front of me

Pre-race Photo Op

while we were throwing horseshoes and my horseshoe hit him in the back of the head. (Talk about a ringer!) Or the time that we were playing a friendly game of baseball on another July 4 holiday at Grandma's – I was batting, and he was playing catcher. Instead of striding into the ball, I moved my back foot back and took a swing. Instead of hitting the ball, again I hit Rocky in the back

3

of the head. I don't remember him needing stitches, but I do know that he didn't need for night to come in order to see stars that July 4th!

On school days Rocky and I would get off the bus after school and quickly do any chores that we had to do and then rush to the barn for our nightly one-on-one game.

The barn had an eleven-foot basket with no net on it, but we didn't care. We played for the state championship every night on that goal. And every night one of us would win the game to 100 by one point. And every night the game ended in a fight because one of us accused the other of double dribbling, travelling, fouling, etc. while making the last basket of the game. And every night mom would have to come out to the barn and separate us, give us a whack, and make us go into the house and clean up for supper. It became a ritual.

After Donnie (that's what mom and us non-cool people called my brother) got into high school and discovered...GIRLS... our nightly one-on-one games ended. As he drove off on his Cushman Eagle Motor Scooter (read ultra-cool here), I would trek to the barn or the garage (we had a six-foot high basket inside the garage that you could dunk on and an eight-foot basket on the outside of the garage) to play imaginary games. (I envisioned myself as the star of the Delphos St. John's Blue Jays. Those gals who were riding on the back of Rocky's Cushman Eagle became my groupies after I hit the imaginary game-winning shot against arch-rival Lima Central Catholic!)

The Junior High Years
"You know that feeling when you meet someone and your heart skips a beat? Yeah, that's arrhythmia. You can die from that!" (Anonymous)

Eventually we moved from the farm in Delphos to a small town about 20 miles away named Ottawa, where I continued to play ball on a basket nailed to our garage and Rocky continued to chase...girls... as a sophomore in high school. When he turned sixteen, he sold his Cushman Eagle and bought the mother

4

lode – a cherry red two door '57 Chevy! His one-on-one days took on a whole new meaning, which I still didn't quite understand at the time. He became the most popular kid in high school while I became the best player on the local Catholic grade school's 6th grade team.

Cool vs. Uncool: Rocky's '57 Chevy parked behind my Nash Rambler as sister Patty poses.

We loved Ottawa. It's where I became "cool" – again, I credit my big brother. He got one of his rich friends to give me a used pair of black loafers (two sizes too big). I wore those black loafers with white sox and thought I was "the cat's ass." (For you younger folks, "the Cat's Ass" in the sixties was the vernacular for meaning you were a stud, the best, the bomb.)

After my eighth-grade year at Ottawa Sts. Peter and Paul, my dad moved us to the big city – Lima, Ohio, a town of about 50,000 people located about 20 miles from Ottawa. I was sad because I had finally discovered why Rocky took such an interest in …girls… and I was deeply in love with Pam Deters, one of the girls in my class who lived about a block from me. (It ended up that it wouldn't have mattered if we had stayed in Ottawa anyway – Pam's parents sent her to an all-girls high school in Toledo after one of the nuns at Sts. Peter and Paul told Pam's parents and my mom that I had been seen sitting next to Pam with my arm around her at the local movie theatre!)

The High School Years

"Train up a child in the way he should go: and when he is old, he will not depart from it." (Proverbs 22:6)

The big city, Lima, was hard for me at first. The only guys I knew in my grade at the high school (Lima Central Catholic, the school I always beat in my imaginary Delphos St. John's days on the farm) were guys who played on Lima's four

Catholic grade school teams – teams our Sts. Peter and Paul teams beat for the 7th and 8th grade area championships. It wasn't that they disliked me; it was just that they had their established friendships and I was the new guy on the block. It didn't help either that they had hit a growth spurt and I still had the body of a 5th grader. I was all of 5'2" tall and weighed less than 100 pounds as a freshman. But I could really shoot it, so I earned a spot as a starting guard on the freshmen basketball team. Unfortunately, the freshmen coach was also the varsity head football coach, and by the time we were playing for the city championship, he moved me out of the line-up and played the freshman football quarterback in my place. After we lost the city championship game to Lima Central Jr. High, I kind of got lost for a while. I started to run with a couple of guys who, shall I say, didn't always do the things that make parents proud. My two best friends were Tommy Davis and Bimbo Taflinger, both very good baseball players and basically good kids, but both very interested in exploring the forbidden fruit of alcohol.

Bimbo's parents were never home at night and Tommy's were at the Knights of Columbus hall, so we'd end up at either house totally unsupervised. If we were at Tommy's, we'd raid his parents' basement refrigerator, which they kept stocked with Pabst Blue Ribbon. If we were at Bimbo's, we'd pool our money and call in an order for a case of beer to be delivered from the local Party Shop. (When the delivery man came to the door, we'd have Bimbo's five-year-old brother, Mikey, take the money to the door and say that his mom and dad had just left. The delivery guy would always take the money and leave the beer! Amazing.) After drinking our forbidden fruit juice we'd go out and just do stupid things – turn over garbage cans, throw stones and break windows, etc. We never did anything very serious, but who knows where it could have led had we continued with this behavior.

Toward the end of my sophomore season, I decided I had to change my ways. I was a substitute on the junior varsity (which contained only sophomores), was still running with Tommy and Bimbo and just wasn't accomplishing things in school or on the court that I should have been. The only good thing was that I was now a huge 5'7" and 120 lbs., which was a giant compared to my freshman year. It was at that point that I decided I would do everything possible to regain my former grade school position of being one of the best basketball players in the area. I stopped drinking and carousing with Tommy and Bimbo, got a YMCA membership, and started praying that I could be as tall as Jesus was when he lived on the earth. (I am positive that Jesus was 5 feet 11 and ¾th inches tall, for miraculously that is what I grew to over the summer between my sophomore and junior years in high school.) By going to the Y every day with my friend, Hal Cattell, and lifting weights that summer (which was a no-no for basketball players back then), I gained 30 pounds in addition to growing nearly 5 inches in height. I also played basketball at least 5 hours every day, be it at the Y or the local playground during the day or outside of a local high school in the evening.

I was supposed to get cut from the varsity my junior year. Four of the five starters were back from the previous year, and they were only going to keep 4 or 5 juniors. Long story short – I not only made the team, I earned a starting position and averaged 10 points a game on a team that had 3 other big scorers. Because of the work I did the previous summer, the stage was set for me to be the first one on either side of our family to have an opportunity to go to college. We couldn't afford it, but with a basketball scholarship I could actually go to college and get an education while being able to continue to play ball. It was a dream, and I had to make it come true by having a good senior season.

I worked hard again the summer between my junior and senior years of high school. Playing half-court at the local playground in the evening with Fred Carver helped me learn how to spin the ball off of a backboard from any angle and score, plus how to throw that clever pass that led to an easy bucket. (Freddie was the local playground hero who never played high school ball but schooled the college players who dared come to his playground after he got off of work.) Mom would let me use her car to drive to the lighted outside courts at night at Lima Shawnee High School to play full court with and against the college guys who played at Ohio State, Dayton, Bowling Green, Purdue and other schools. It allowed me to gain the confidence needed to know that I could compete against college-level talent. And when I wasn't sacking groceries during the day at Kroger's, I would make my way to the playground and work on my shooting in between games of four square and checkers (at which I still always won). It was truly the 'Life of Riley' that summer.

Unfortunately, my senior year started with an injury. In pre-season workouts, since the coach was not allowed to be in the gym with the team, I, being the team captain (our other captain was playing football) led the workouts, including the warm-up exercises.

I don't know if anyone does these any more or not, but we used to have to do "leg-lifts" in calisthenics. (A leg-lift is when you lie flat on your back with your legs together, lift your feet simultaneously six inches off the ground, spread your legs while maintaining the six-inch clearance, bring your legs back together, and then lower them to the ground before starting the process over

Coach Clark and 1965-66 LCC T-Birds

VARSITY BASKETBALL TEAM – Kneeling from L to R : Pat McCormick, Steve Riepenhoff, Bill Wade, Dave Moran, and Denny Cullen. Standing from L to R : Joe Brickner, Rich Thompson, Bob Seggerson, Coach William Clark, Roger Fisher, John Savakalitis, and Tony Quatman.

again. If you are having trouble envisioning this, imagine making a "snow angel" in the snow on the ground, only you lift your legs up six inches instead of scraping them along the ground.) I decided one day to show our team what it meant to be tough, so we did leg-lifts until everyone dropped but me. I personified the Energizer Bunny - I kept going and going. I finally stopped, and we finished our basketball workout. The next day I couldn't bend over. I had severely strained my back, and it would be quite some time before I was even able to tie my shoes. The school sent me to doctors, therapists, etc., but nothing would help. By the time our season started I still couldn't bend over and pick up a ball. Eight games into the season (of an 18-game schedule) I was playing about 1.5 quarters a game, averaging about 4 or 5 points and being a non-factor in games. At half-time they'd put a heating device on my back, but it wouldn't make much difference the second half. I prayed hard for healing. Finally, I went to an osteopath and after two sessions of being twisted and turned every which way but loose, I was healed! For the remainder of the year I averaged over 18 points per game and was able to pass the way I used to pass before the injury. Unfortunately, my overall 14 ppg average for the year wasn't anything special – guards like that were a dime a dozen in Ohio. I really wanted to go to Dayton, where my former teammate Dan Sadlier had gone, or to Miami of Ohio. Well, Dayton wasn't interested, and Miami of Ohio reviewed a film where I had 20 points and 19 assists and said, "We aren't interested in the guard, but who is the 6'5" kid he is passing to?" This was the worst thing they could have done. They not only rejected me, they inquired about one of my best friends, Roger "Seymour" Fisher, who could not play a lick! (In the film I sent, Roger had his career high – 24 points on 12 layup assists that I dished out to him!) Needless to say, to this day Roger still reminds me of his 24 to my high game of 23 and how Miami didn't really think much of me but was interested in "Seymour"! (To be fair to Roger, after he enrolled at St. Louis University on an academic scholarship, they asked him to play on SLU's freshman basketball team, which he did.)

The College Years

"Education is the best provision for life's journey." (Aristotle, Ancient Greek philosopher and scientist)

With no big school offers available, I turned to another best friend, Dan Dugan. Dan's father, John, had given me his card after one of my good games my junior year and told me to call him if I was interested in going to college in Kansas. I had opportunities from a number of small colleges in Ohio, but the Kansas school Mr. Dugan was representing, St. Benedict's, had Mr. Dugan's oldest son, Jack, playing for it. Jack Dugan was a very good 6' 5" forward who played three years earlier at Lima Central Catholic. He could have gone to a number of NCAA D-1 schools, but chose St. Benedict's, an all-guys school and his father's alma mater. Mr. Dugan told me that they were a small college power and had an all-American returning. (I think he also mentioned that there was an all-girls school right across town in Atchison!) In fact, the entire team was back from a 19-7 team, and they were going to be pretty good the next year.

Again, to make a long story short, I ended up signing at St. Benedict's College and taking a 24-hour train trip to Atchison, Kansas in August of 1966 to enroll for my first semester of college. Since the school was so far away, I did not make a visit before signing with them. You can understand my anxiety when the train stopped in what appeared to be the middle of nowhere (Armour, MO) and dropped off about 30 soon-to-be freshmen from Ohio, Indiana and Illinois. We were met by hay trucks! We took our bags and belongings and loaded them on the beds of the hay trucks, jumped on the back and held on for dear life as we rode four miles to the bridge over the Missouri River to our final destination, St. Benedict's College. Since I had never been more than 3 hours away from Lima, I was thinking I made the biggest mistake of my life. I was sure that I'd see covered wagons in downtown Atchison and expected the dorms to be made out of logs!

To my surprise, when we got to campus, I found a beautiful school built on the bluffs overlooking the Missouri River. I fell in love with the place, a love that has lasted over 50 years. More than just the beauty of the campus, the hospitality and caring attitude of the Benedictine monks and sisters (at the girls' school, which I frequented a bit) solidified that love that I initially felt for Benedict's. They were, and still are, wonderful people. It is easy to see why the Benedictine Order has lasted over 1500 years.

From a basketball standpoint, I couldn't have made a better decision. The Ravens

The beginning of lifelong relationships.

were indeed talented, and the players became life-long friends. I was fortunate enough to beat out some upperclassmen and settled in as the 8th man on a team that won the 1967 NAIA National Championship. We went 27-2 and won our last 19 in a row. I got to play in the first half of most games, mainly because we had a comfortable lead. (Our average winning margin that year was 19 points per game.) I was the fourth guard in Coach Ralph Nolan's 3-guard rotation! Regardless, that season taught me more about what it takes to win than any other experience I've had. I lost 15 pounds and actually learned how to play defense that season! Those lessons allowed me to play on subsequent teams that were national champions at every age division. Shoot, our St. Louis Kutis Funeral Home team (yes, funeral home sponsorship – you think they were betting on the come?) not only won the 1976 NABA National Championship, we even won the 1998 Nike World Games' "45 and over" basketball championship in Portland against Russia. What a great feeling of accomplishment, even if it was 45 and over. I was the player-coach on many of these after-college championship teams, so it was doubly satisfying for me.

Entering Real Life

> *"The difference between school and life? In school, you are taught a lesson and then given a test. In life, you are given a test that teaches you a lesson!"* *(Tom Bodett, American voice actor {Motel 6})*

During my senior year at Benedict's I interviewed on campus with Southwestern Bell Telephone Company (SWB - now the new AT&T). I told them that I was a

math major, the captain of our basketball team as a junior and senior, was the president of the letterman's club as a senior and was married to a "Mountie" from the Atchison all-girls school, Mt. St. Scholastica. It was my first and only job interview. Having to blow my own horn in the interview made me feel like an arrogant jerk, and I left the interview thinking they would

Teammate and roommate Steve Northcraft on graduation day.

never hire me. (That was okay, because I had been awarded assistantships at Colorado State and Oklahoma State in their MBA programs, so I wouldn't need a job anyway, I thought.) Much to my surprise, a job offer came in the spring of 1970. It was very timely, and God was looking out for me and my family, for my wife was pregnant with our first son and I really needed a job. I also needed to get a high lottery number if I didn't want to go to Viet Nam after graduation. Unfortunately, my lottery number was 141. It might as well have been #1. It was the first draft lottery, and they went all the way up to 195 before they had enough to populate the needs of the military that year.

(For those of you who did not live through these times, the Vietnam War was very unpopular. None of the young people wanted to go to "Nam." It wasn't a case of not wanting to serve your country – rather it was a case of "why are we over there anyway. They didn't do anything to us." It was much worse than the attitude shown by some when the U.S. entered Iraq recently.) Fortunately for me and about two-thirds of my classmates, the Kansas National Guard had been activated for the war and was completing their active duty in the spring of 1970. A large number of positions, therefore, were open at various National Guard units, including the Infantry unit in Atchison. The rush to sign up was reminiscent of the rush we made when Atchison's Red Rooster Bar would have 25 cent pitcher night! Thus, after graduation in May 1970 from St. Benedict's, I took a detour to the tropical paradise known as Ft. Polk, Louisiana, prior to joining SW Bell's Initial Management Development Program (IMDP).

If college is the best four years of your life (which they are), then the 5 months I

With army buddy Sam Cash at a Fort Puke barracks

spent at Ft. Puke in basic training and Advanced Infantry Training were the worst 5 months of my life. I was separated from my wife and newborn son, I was physically miserable in the heat, humidity, and mosquito infested army base, and I hated the way the drill sergeants treated people. But you learned quickly to keep your mouth shut, do as you are told and count the days until you get out. Knowing you were going back to Kansas and not going to Viet Nam, like all the regular army guys who were your buddies in camp, made it bearable. Sure enough, in late October 1970, I loaded up our 1962 Chevy with my wife, my son Alex, and our few belongings and drove from her parents' home in Baytown, Texas to Wichita, Kansas to begin a nearly 28-year career with SWB.

Chapter 1: The Business Career: building the financial and educational foundations

"It is not the beauty of a building you should look at; it's the construction of the foundation that will stand the test of time." (David Allan Coe, American country & western singer and songwriter)

n order to have even the remotest opportunity to become a college coach, there were a number of "prerequisites" that had to come to fruition for me. Key among these was to have enough money saved to be able to take a huge reduction in salary, and secondly to have an advanced degree that would make me attractive from a college instructor's standpoint.

Good Job. Good Pay.

"Work to become, not to acquire." (Elbert Hubbard, American writer, publisher, artist, and philosopher.)

The path that I followed to get the opportunity to live my "Dream" (i.e., dream of coaching) started with getting a good job with a good company – Southwestern Bell Telephone Company. Back in 1970, businesses did a majority of their hiring for career managers by visiting college campuses. They were trying to find good matches for the job opportunities they had projected for their company for the next 5 years or so. SWB, one of the largest subsidiaries of AT&T at the time, visited St. Benedict's in the fall of 1969. The Vietnam War was going full force and young business talent was projected to get scarcer due to the number of young men who would be required to enter the armed services after the upcoming initial draft lottery. Back in 1970, businesses only recruited men for these management positions. Women were not considered to have "career" interests in the business world. So, when I got hired by SWB I joined about 15 other young men in SWB's Kansas Initial Management Development Program (IMDP, pronounced im-dip). We were spread among the various functional departments of the company, and I was assigned to the Wichita Accounting Department (I guess because I majored in math.). The IMDP program (the "old heads" at SWB had a ball with that acronym – especially the "dip" part) was a high risk, high reward management program. (After one year you were either fired or promoted.) All IMDP's reported directly to a third level manager in their specific functional area. After attending a week-long management training session where you learned about Peter Drucker and the other management gurus of the day, you were thrown directly into a supervising position with no training at all in the specific function. The theory was you would either sink or swim, depending upon your personality, ingenuity, work ethic, and management skills. After one year the company would decide to keep you or not. You were expected to be able to handle third level management positions within five years. The decision to keep you with the company was based on management's assessment of your being able to handle that level of responsibility after observing how well you managed the first year on the job.

My first assignment was to be the Payroll Unit Supervisor for the southern half of SWB's Kansas operations. I had eight direct reports, all women. All but one had at least 25 years' service with the company. Most, but not all, were nice. I remember my first day on the job - my boss, Max Birt, simply walked me to the payroll unit and showed me my desk and walked out. (That was the IMDP way.) He didn't introduce me to the gals or anything. It was up to me to introduce myself to a unit of experienced workers who would now be reporting to this wet-behind-the-ears kid. They were really nice about making me feel welcome. They had gone through this exercise before and knew that I wouldn't be around too long. After a week or so I started feeling a little comfortable in my environment. Once again, I thought I was the "cat's ass" - coming out of college and making a staggering $800 per month, owning two new suits, a plethora of impressive new ties and driving a slightly used 1970 Chevy Impala! I thought I had it made – until God decided to put me in my place.

Back in those days the clerical offices were set up such that the desks all faced one direction in one big room. The supervisor's desk was at the back of the room so that the employees couldn't see you unless they turned around. I guess this was done so that employees assumed that they were always being watched - so they couldn't "screw off" without being caught. One day I was sitting in my chair with my feet up on my desk just taking in how cool I was when all of sudden the chair tipped over backward. I came crashing to the floor with my feet in the air and my pride in my back pocket. All eight gals turned around to see what the loud crash was only to see the chair tipped over and their new supervisor flat on his back. I'm sure they were laughing hysterically inside, but they had the graciousness to only chuckle a little while coming to see if I was alright. The only thing broken was my pride, which was a lesson I have carried with me for the rest of my life.

After "surviving" the Payroll Unit assignment and a second assignment seven months into my career where I had 21 direct reports (20 women), I passed the one-year test and was promoted to the job of Evening and Night Manager in the Computer Room at SWB's Topeka Accounting Office. (In those days there was no IT organization. Computers were a new business asset, and the Accounting Department assumed the management and supervision of all computer functions that related to report generation.) I was now a second level manager who had two first-level managers reporting to me – one ran the evening shift and one ran the night shift. Realize that I did not know the first thing about computers, but again, if you were an IMDP...

I remember walking into the computer room with my new boss the first night and saying "Hey, that is a great looking computer!" to which he replied, "There are three computers out there." (Now you can see why the "old heads" emphasized the "dip" part of IMDP.)

After Hours Fun?

"Whatever you can do or dream you can, begin it. Boldness has genius, power, and magic in it." (Johann Wolfgang Goethe, German writer and statesman)

It was on this job that I got my first inspiration to further my formal education. Bell was really good at sending you to training classes once you completed your first IMDP year, and I attended many computer classes and learned a lot. Bell also had a tuition reimbursement program as part of their benefit package. You could take a business-related class and if you received a "C" or above the company would reimburse you for the cost of tuition for the course. One day a programmer from St. Louis Headquarters came to visit Topeka to help us through a computer conversion project and during one of our breaks he told me about an MBA program at Southern Illinois University at Edwardsville, Ill. It was a night program that enabled you to earn an MBA in 18 to 24 months. I always wanted to get an MBA but thought it wouldn't be possible working full time. No university close to Topeka offered such a program, so it was exciting to know that if I ever got transferred to St. Louis, I could pursue the MBA at SIU–E. This would eventually play a critical role not only in my career path at SWB, but also in positioning myself to be an attractive candidate for my Dream Job (Coaching) later in life.

Bell's method of developing managers in those days entailed moving their managers to not only different jobs but also to different locations about every two years or so. Like clockwork, about three years into my career I was moved to St. Louis Headquarters to the programming staff to work on a new Billing System. Again, I did not know how to program, but Bell sent me to classes to learn how to code in Assembler Language. (Assembler was as close to machine language as you could get – it pre-dated COBOL, DOS, etc.) While on this job I was able to enroll in the MBA Program at SIU-E, just like I had hoped I would back in Topeka. I was able to get an MBA in 18 months, but it wasn't easy.

My wife at that time also wanted to get a master's degree in Human Services, so she would drive downtown and pick me up at 5 p.m. and we would drive to SIU-E. We'd drop her off at her class, which started at 5:30 p.m. By then we had two sons, so the boys and I would eat a pre-made dinner in the car and then drive to a sitter in Edwardsville. After dropping them off, I'd return to campus, park the car in a pre-designated area, and then go to my 6:30 p.m. class. My wife would get out of class at 8:30 p.m., get the car and pick up the boys, then drive back to campus and pick me up after I got out at 9:30 p.m. We'd then drive to St. Louis, pick up my car at work, and drive home. We would do this two, and sometimes three, times a week for a year and a half. It was a hectic schedule, but by studying at lunch and on weekends, I was able to graduate in 1976 with a Master's in Business Administration.

New Opportunities From Advanced Degree

"For I know the plans I have for you" – this is the Lord's declaration – "plans for your welfare, not for disaster, to give you a future and a hope." (Jeremiah 29:11)

The MBA opened doors for me. Shortly after receiving the degree I interviewed for a job in the Treasury Department at SWB. Fortunately for me the man who interviewed me was not one who judged by looks but rather by other attributes. Back in 1976 long hair was the style for men. Well, I had to be in style. My hair

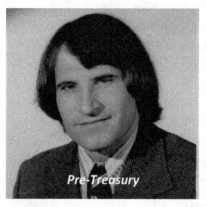
Pre-Treasury

was down to my shoulders. I showed up for an interview (in probably the most traditional functional Department in probably the most traditional company in the U.S.) with hair that looked like Fabio! Don George, the Assistant Treasurer and interviewer, hired me anyway. I'm sure he was shocked (and relieved) when I showed up the first day on the new job with short, well-groomed hair.

Getting to Treasury was another critical step in my being able to become a coach later in life, as you will see later in the book. It was also a breath of fresh air – I had a great job and worked for a great boss. I was in charge of "mechanizing" Treasury, which meant using computers for functions they did by hand. The department was headed by a wonderful man – Treasurer Art Seewoester.

Everybody loved "Mr. See." Where the Accounting department was full of politics and one-ups-manship, Treasury was a place where people liked each other and worked together to do the best job possible. I credit this attitude to Mr. See and to Don George, who followed in Mr. See's ways. I learned so much about behavioral leadership from these two men, and it was mostly by simply observing how they treated people and how they got things done.

Post-Treasury

Unsuspected Roadblock

> *"Cast your burden on the Lord, and he will support you; He will never allow the righteous to be shaken." (Psalm 55:22)*

After about two years at Treasury Headquarters mechanizing the check reconciliation process, Mr. George promoted me to the Treasury Manager

18

position back in Topeka. This was my first third-level job, and I was thrilled. Unfortunately, my personal life hadn't progressed as well. I had gone through a divorce in St. Louis, and for about a year had struggled to make sense out of a life that had taken a turn I hadn't expected. Fortunately, I was awarded custody of my two sons, and fortunately I worked for Don George.

In the middle of a horrendous conversion of the check reconciliation process, Don's wife Joanna would pick up the boys (5 and 7) from school, take them home and feed them supper and keep them until I could leave work and pick them up by 9 or 10 p.m. (The Georges personified what Jesus said when he talked about feeding and clothing your neighbor, etc. They are saints.) Some nights I would drive to the George's south St. Louis house, pick up the boys and return to the office to work on the check processing conversion. The kids loved it, for they would play "Army Ranger" and crawl from the back of the room under all the desks and make a "sneak attack" with the myriad of rubber bands we had in the check processing unit. They'd shoot those

Alex and Scott

rubber bands at me, I'd scream like I was mortally wounded, and they'd scurry out of the office laughing at how inept I was at being able to discover their sneak attacks. Within minutes they'd be back crawling from the back of the room again plotting to wipe out the enemy who foolishly had his back to them as he was keying in information at the desk in the front of the room. We did this routine for quite some time until one night they decided to have a hallway race with the clerical chairs from the office. At the time I worked on the 29th floor of SWB's 1010 Pine Headquarters Building, a beautiful Gothic structured masterpiece that contained marble floors and walls. The marble hallway made a great racetrack for the wheeled desk chairs, but the marble kickboard did not make for a soft landing for Alex after he flew off a racing chair headfirst. After "the enemy" took Alex to the emergency room for multiple stitches, Joann George would no longer let me pick up the boys and

19

bring them back to the office – they were at the George's home until Dad came to take them home!

Silver Lining

"Now if any of you lacks wisdom, he should ask God, who gives to all generously and without criticizing, and it will be given to him." *(James 1:5)*

The new job in Topeka gave me a fresh lease on life. I was able to live literally 10 minutes from work, 5 minutes from the boys' school, 5 minutes from the Y – you get the picture. I could be a single dad thoroughly involved in my sons' lives while still being totally engaged at work. Since the boys were now 6 and 8 years old, I could take them to city league basketball games or weekend basketball road trips, and they would be perfectly happy running under the bleachers chasing all the other little kids at the games. By working out every day at lunchtime at the Y, I was able to stay in competitive basketball shape. It was truly a blessing to be sent to Topeka – and we stayed there for 13 years.

The best part, though, of moving to Topeka was meeting my future wife, Connie. She was a recent college graduate who had worked for Bell for about three years. She worked for the Accounting General Manager in Topeka, so I got to see her at work often, since I had to coordinate with the Accounting GM. After having been previously married for eight years, I had found it awkward to date in St. Louis. It seemed like there was always baggage involved in every relationship, including my own baggage. Connie was different. She had never been married, she was Catholic, she had career aspirations, she was honest, and she was very well grounded. (Oh yes, she was a "fox" too.) Our first date was a lunch at which we discussed a fascinating mini-series on TV that Easter season called "Jesus of Nazareth." To this day, it is still one of our favorite movies.

When I left St. Louis, I had told my boss that I was no longer mobile. I wanted my sons to grow up in Topeka where they were surrounded by wonderful, caring people. Everyone thinks that being a single dad is very difficult, but I found that living in Topeka made being a single dad rather easy. It was amazing how the moms at the grade school where the boys went to school would go so far out of their way to help make life easier for the boys and me. Carpools, dinners, watching the kids if I had to work – any way they could help, they would. Single dads were rather rare back then, I guess, and I know they felt sorry for me. I must admit, I let them feel that way – shoot, I loved the attention too!

My plan was to stay in Topeka until both sons graduated from high school.

The day I tricked her.

Six months in I was offered a promotion to a really good career opportunity at AT&T in New York, but I said no. Six months later I was offered another promotion, back to St. Louis, and again I said no. (Those turned out to be the two best decisions I made concerning my career and my family.) I wasn't offered anything again for twelve years – which was perfect.

I had also decided that I would not get married again until the boys graduated from high school, even though the Catholic Church had annulled my first marriage and I was free to marry again. Funny how that plan didn't work out. I did hold out for six years. It is amazing that Connie didn't tell me to take a hike during that time – God must have dulled her thinking during those years. Finally, I wised up and we got married (and have been now for over 36 years).

The Final Bell Career Move

"When you delegate tasks, you create followers. When you delegate authority, you create leaders." (Craig Groeschel, founder and senior pastor of Life.Church)

After my youngest son, Scott, graduated from high school, I informed my boss (now Bob Steinmetz) that I was once again mobile. About six months later I accepted a job back in St. Louis as the third level manager in charge of cash management and banking for the telephone company. (The company was going through significant downsizing and my job was being eliminated in Kansas. It is so interesting to realize how God's plan works. The downsizing didn't take place until Scott had graduated from high school, or about 13 years after I said that I would be immobile for 13 years.) The new job was great, and Connie got a job in

21

Payroll in St. Louis, so we were able to sell the home in Topeka and build a new one in South St. Louis County. Again, the timing couldn't have been better.

About a year after I went to St. Louis my boss, the Assistant Treasurer, took an early buy-out and I was promoted into his position. It was the best job I had in all of my twenty-seven plus years at Bell. I reported to the CFO & Treasurer, who spent all of his time on the accounting and financial planning side and allowed me the freedom to act as the Treasurer. I had a crack staff, most of whom, like me, loved to pursue new and better ways of doing things. We became not only the best Bell Treasury group in the U.S.; we also became one of the best Treasury organizations in the land, regardless of the industry. (Back in the 90's companies were really into benchmarking, and we were constantly being visited by other companies and being asked to talk at Treasury industry forums about our leading-edge processes.) It was really fun, and personally rewarding.

Two For Two at Education U

"Think about Him in all your ways, and He will guide you on the right paths." (Proverbs 3:6)

It was during my time as Assistant Treasurer that another milestone on my way to coaching was achieved. Similar to when I worked in St. Louis the first time, on my second St. Louis tour I had decided to return to school once more and work on my doctorate. I wanted to be able to teach at the college level after I retired, and I thought a doctorate would put me in a position to do just that. Webster University had a program that was only offered on their home campus in St. Louis where you could actually earn a Doctor of Applied Management degree and still have a job during the day. All classes were offered at night in four-hour blocks.

Team Graduation: Connie got her Master's, I got my Doctorate

I applied and was accepted pending my passing a graduate level marketing class, which I did. Our class of 24 began in 1992, but only twelve of us completed the grueling course schedule. At the end of the formal classes, we had to take an 8-hour, "one and done" comprehensive exam. It was brutal, and only 6 of us passed, which meant the other six wasted more than two years of their life taking formal classes. Passing the exam only got you half-way, though. You had four years in which to complete your dissertation, or else you would not be allowed to continue to work on it. Needless to say, it didn't take long for me to start my research and begin to work on the document. After two years of research and writing, I passed two review boards and successfully defended my study and was awarded my doctorate in 1996. This was the final piece that was needed in opening the door to my coaching dream, although I didn't know it at the time.

Say What?

"A successful man is one who can lay a firm foundation from the bricks that others throw at him." (David Brinkley, American newscaster)

The final career move that allowed the dream to happen occurred when SW Bell bought Pacific Bell in 1996. (For those of you who are unfamiliar with the history of AT&T or are too young to remember, the federal government broke AT&T up into 7 separate companies in 1984. All seven were still big enough to be considered a Fortune 50 company. After the '84 divestiture, SBC, as Southwestern Bell became known, eventually started to buy up parts or all of other AT&T divested companies. They eventually even bought the remnant of AT&T itself and adopted its name.) As companies do when they merge, Bell eliminated the duplicate jobs. This is always stressful for people in Finance and other "Overhead" functions. There is no need for two accounting groups, or two treasury groups, or two benefit groups, etc. SW Bell took it one step further. SWB was the telephone subsidiary of SBC, making up about 90% of the corporation back then (wireless made up the remainder). Being the holding company and having a staff at corporate headquarters in San Antonio, Texas, SBC decided to not only eliminate Pac Bell's overhead departments, they decided to merge some of SWB's departments into San Antonio also. Treasury was one of those groups. So after about a year of planning, the Assistant Treasurer's position and staff at SWB was merged into San Antonio's Assistant Treasurer's organization and I was out of a job. I worked for a brief time on the company merger team, and then was assigned the Executive Director of Billing position for SWB. I had been in Billing many, many years earlier, but after moving into Finance in 1976, I had lost all interest in IT, and Billing in particular. Needless to say, my bubble burst as far as SWB's perfect job was concerned. Unbeknownst to me, God was working His plan.

Meanwhile, while I was working on my doctorate, a 1968 St. Benedict's grad by the name of Dr. Dan Carey became president of Benedictine College (BC), the name St. Benedict's and Mt. St. Scholastica adopted when the two schools merged in 1971. Dan was a great basketball fan while in college and a very good student who knew how to have a good time, too. He epitomized the typical "Raven" of the 60's and had gone on and been very successful in Catholic higher education after graduating from Benedict's.

Each year as I was progressing through the doctoral program Dan would call me and ask me if I was interested in coming to BC to teach in the business department after I earned my degree. I would tell him that I would certainly do that after I retired, which Bell would allow their managers to do with a full pension at age 55. (I was 43 in 1991 when I started on my doctorate.) He'd say "great" and then call me the next year. This went on until 1998, when a different twist was thrown into the offer. He called me in March with the same question. I gave the same answer. He then said, "Would it make any difference if we made you the head men's basketball coach as well as having you teach a course or two in the business school?" I about dropped the phone (which would have been preferable to tipping over backwards in my chair again). About a year earlier I had had lunch in Atchison with one of Dr. Carey's cabinet members, and in a casual conversation he asked, "If there was anything you could do that you wanted to do, what would it be?" I told him, like a million other people would, that I would like to coach. We then discussed the basketball program at BC and how I thought certain changes could be made to help them be successful. We had a nice conversation, but I never thought about it again – until that day in March when Dr. Carey called. It so happened that the current basketball coach resigned and in discussing candidates with the President, this cabinet member related his luncheon discussion with me from the previous year. Dan made a couple of calls to

24

determine how valid my coaching credentials were, thought they were appropriate, and then called me and made the offer.

Safe Or Sorry?

"Do not be too timid and squeamish about your actions. All life is an experiment." (Ralph Waldo Emerson, American essayist, lecturer, philosopher, and poet.)

Now I faced the situation that many of us never get the chance to face – do you chase the dream or settle for the comfort and security of a well-paying job? All kinds of obstacles raced through my head. Can I afford to change careers; what will my wife do if she can't get a transfer to the KC area; can we sell the house, and will it bring what it is worth on the market; do I know enough about the game to coach at the college level, etc. The first thing I did was to call my wife, Connie, and discussed it with her.

{Let me insert here just how important it is to have a supportive spouse if you plan to be a coach. My wife made major sacrifices for me to be able to pursue my dream of coaching. Ironically, simultaneous to the coaching position being offered to me, she was offered a job in SW Bell's St. Louis employment office. Even though she liked the Benefits group she was working in in downtown St. Louis, she wanted badly to get back to the employment office to a job like she had in Topeka when we left there in 1991. She literally had to turn down the St. Louis employment office job offer so that I could become a coach. It didn't stop there either, to which the spouses of all coaches will attest. Sometimes you must feel like a widow(er) when your spouse is a coach. Your spouse will be gone many, many nights during the season, either at games, practices, scouting or recruiting. Your spouse will probably be preoccupied mentally and not show much attention to you during the season. Many social plans will have to be set aside due to your spouse's schedule. The list goes on and on. My point is, unless you get buy-in from your spouse, your dream job could turn into a marital nightmare!}

Connie knew how much I loved basketball and how unhappy I had become in my current job at Bell. We decided that even though I didn't have much time to decide, we would pray about it for a few days. After praying and soul searching, we put together a mental plan that would have to take place in order for me to be able to accept the Benedictine offer.

The first thing I had to do was approach my boss, a different CFO than the one I worked for as the Assistant Treasurer, and see if there was any chance I could get a buyout. (We were downsizing significantly due to the PacBell merger and there were many SWB managers being forced to accept buyouts who wanted to continue working.) The next thing we had to do was explore the opportunities for Connie at SWB in KC. (As mentioned earlier, she worked in Benefits and there was no benefit organization in KC.) I also had to verify that I had to reach age 50 with SWB or else I would lose my opportunity for a discounted pension. (I would turn 50 in mid-August 1998.) Amazingly, it had to be God's will, for

Retirement Party Decorative Cake

everything fell into place. I was able to recommend a replacement for me who had Billing IT experience, was on the short list, and wanted to stay. The CFO agreed to the two of us swapping positions – he retained the Billing IT job at Bell, and I got a buyout package. Connie found a position in KC and was transferred there, and get this, included was the company's guarantee to buy our house in St. Louis if we couldn't sell it! (This was part of the management transfer plan at SWB.) Finally, I had to get to my 50th birthday in order to qualify for a discounted pension – which my boss agreed to do. So, on August 18, 1998, I officially retired from Southwestern Bell with over 27 years of service and began a new career in coaching as Head Men's Basketball Coach at Benedictine College – MY DREAM JOB!

So, You Want to Be a Coach … Lesson #1:
In order to be available when the "Dream Job" opportunity presents itself, strive to pre-build the foundation required to be a candidate. Also, ensure your spouse understands the sacrifices he/she will have to make being the spouse of a coach, and is willing to make those sacrifices.

Chapter 2: The Athletic Career: building the basketball resume

"The best way to predict the future is to create it." (Abraham Lincoln, 16th president of the United States)

Being a good player is not enough to become a good coach in any sport. In fact, there are many good coaches who were not good players or even players at all (e.g., Scott Drew at Baylor, Bruce Pearl at Auburn). However, I do believe that it helps to have played the game if you want to be a coach, for there is nothing like experiencing the heat of battle that creates an imprint on your mind as to what it takes to be successful in the heat of that battle.

The Beginning Of The Love Affair

"Desire! That is the one secret of every man's career. Not education. Not being born with hidden talents. Desire." (Johnny Carson, American comedian)

I had mentioned earlier that I had probably chosen basketball over football and baseball simply because I was better at it than I was at the other two. However, there may be more to it than that - I don't remember the first time I played football or baseball, but I do remember the first time I shot a basketball.

Grandma's garage about 3 years before I got hooked.

My brother introduced me to the game one day in Grandma's and Grandpa's driveway on the farm when I was about 5 years old. They had a single, stand-alone garage in which they parked their only car - a 1951 Hudson, I think. On the front of the garage someone had nailed up a basket. My memory is of my brother shooting baskets one day, and like always, I wanted to do everything my older brother did. So, he let me shoot a couple of times, and I remember how cool it was when the ball went through the net-less rim. I wasn't strong enough to shoot overhand, so I was shooting underhand! It didn't matter – as long the ball went through the hoop, the thrill was there. And it still is. Playing pick-up or old men's tournaments, "lacing "one from the deep corner still sends that sensation of accomplishment through your veins.

My first recollection of a league was at Delphos St. John's in the third grade Saturday morning half-court league. I would wait all week anticipating the Saturday morning games. We were divided into teams and played on eight-foot baskets nailed to the side walls of the upstairs auditorium at the grade school. The smell of basketball shoes (although we always called them tennis shoes, or rather, "tennashoes") in the little room where all the third graders would put on their uniforms and shoes before playing was a smell that really got the adrenalin going for me. The more well-to-do kids wore Chuck Taylor Converse All-Stars – we less fortunate kids wore Red Ball Jets. It didn't matter to any of us though, as long as we got to play. Since we had then moved to the rented farmhouse with the three baskets I had mentioned earlier, one of which was an eight-foot jobby on our garage, I was pretty accurate at hitting perimeter shots at the grade school "gym." This only reinforced my love for playing basketball.

Playing full court games did not happen until after we had moved to Ottawa while I was in the sixth grade.

It's funny now remembering how one time when I returned to Grandma's for a visit after we had moved to Ottawa, I had Bobby Speiles, my best friend and a neighboring farm boy, come over to Grandma's so that I could show him how I could now dribble behind my back. (You knew a kid was your best friend when you could ride your bikes down a country road together singing at the top of your lungs "Bye-Bye Love" by the Everly Brothers.) Since all the courts we played on outside at the farm were on gravel, I had to take him over to the cistern and show him my great dribbling technique on the concrete that covered the cistern! (My driveway in Ottawa was concrete, so I'm sure that is where I learned to dribble so that the ball didn't veer off in other directions like it did on our rut-laced driveways on the farm.)

At Ottawa I also was exposed to and got hooked on the publicity that surrounds athletics in America. The local newspaper was published every Thursday, as I recall. If you can believe it, the paper covered our sixth-grade games. I still recall seeing the bold print stating that "Brickner scores 21 in Sts. Peter and Paul's 33-28 road win." My wife says I crave attention (although I disagree, as you would expect), and I guess this was the start of that. Seeing your name in print is ego-boosting, no doubt. Sports are one of the few positive ways to actually get your name in the paper, and starting in the sixth grade, I was fortunate enough to be able to experience that boost. It was to continue throughout high school, college, and even after college for me.

Mentors

"Be imitators of me, just as I also am of Christ." (1 Corinthians 11:1)

Playing basketball was always fun for me, but I also approached the game from a tactical standpoint. I was fortunate enough to have some pretty good coaches as I was growing up. The ones I liked the best were the ones who were positive, even when you made a mistake. My experiences in the sixth, seventh and eighth grade years in Ottawa laid a foundation for me in how I would try to coach in the future. Our coaches were tough from the standpoint of expecting you to execute the way you were taught, but they weren't screamers. They were positive people who instilled confidence in me. My dad, who was not involved in athletics, had a short temper and little patience. I loved my dad, but I didn't like doing things with him because if you made a mistake he'd get angry and "chastise" you. My coaches were different, and I gravitated to them and their ways of motivating. Had they not been that way, I probably would have never pursued basketball or coaching.

My high school years were spent playing for Bill Clark, a History teacher with a big voice, a bigger heart, and a great sense of humor. Mr. Clark wasn't a skilled basketball coach from a tactical standpoint, but he gave his all for us. He was a great History teacher who happened to coach basketball as a favor to our principal at Lima Central Catholic, Father E.C. Herr. (Fr. Herr was a short man with a big voice too - and a short temper. He was so good, though, to so many at LCC. For example, knowing my family could not afford to buy me contacts my junior year, he got a doctor friend of his to "donate" a pair of hard lens contacts to me so that I did not have to play ball in cumbersome glasses.)

Coach Clark taught me the value of finding light moments in life, even when things weren't going your way.

I remember playing in a tight game my senior year when Coach Clark called a timeout late in the game and we had the ball with the game tied. One of my teammates, Pat McCormick, a really good football player with the energy of two people, was a starting forward and leading rebounder for us even though he was only 6 feet tall and weighed 170 pounds. Pat was not a great shooter, probably because he played at warp speed. In the huddle, Coach Clark set up a play and his last words were "and for God's sake, don't pass the ball to McCormick – he'll throw it over the backboard!" To say the least, it cracked us up. To be honest, I don't remember if we made the shot or not, but what I do remember is that it relaxed us to the point of not being too nervous to execute – all done because of Coach's sense of humor. It was a lesson that I carried with me not only into business and coaching, but also into life in general.

My college coaches were the most influential as it concerns my approach to practicing, playing, and eventually coaching the game. My four years at St. Benedict's were under the tutelage of Ralph Nolan, a NAIA Hall of Fame coach, and his assistant, Tom Colwell. They made a pretty good team – Nolan was normally the calm, collected one and Colwell was the driver.

Point guard instructions.

In his last game as coach at St. Benedict's, Ralph Nolan gave some advice to Joe Brickner in the NAIA tournament in 1978. The Ravens, lost the game to Central Washington, ending Nolan's 24 year stint at the Atchison school.

Ravens' Nolan still calm, quiet

During my freshman year, when we won the NAIA National Championship, Nolan didn't do a lot of on-court coaching in practice. He would normally stand on the sideline smoking a cigarette (yep – a cigarette at practice), while Colwell would do most of the coaching. Periodically Nolan would step in and make a point, or call a player over to emphasize a concept, but normally he'd just observe while smoking or counting his change! When it came game time, though, Nolan called the shots. His ability not to get too excited, regardless of the situation, taught me to stay calm even in the toughest of situations. Since I was his point guard, it was very important that I was able to keep my head

30

while on the court and simultaneously calm my teammates, if needed. This attribute was something that was beneficial to me especially in the business world – overreacting can be the death knell in many situations. I also found myself emulating this behavior once I became a college coach.

Colwell taught me to never give up. He was a very good fundamentals teacher, and he would make you believe that once you mastered the fundamental, no one could beat you, regardless of their talent level. It came down to their talent against your knowledge and will, and he would not allow you to fail. Coach Colwell wasn't necessarily a screamer, but he was very tough and never smiled. Interestingly, though, we all loved him, for he had a knack of making you know that he wasn't attacking you personally when he was making his point – he was only trying to make you better. That is a rare skill and one that I tried to emulate but was never certain that I mastered.

Honing The Skills

"Great things are not done by impulse, but by a series of small things brought together." (Vincent van Gogh, Dutch post-impressionist painter)

After graduating from college and going to work for Bell, I continued to play ball in city leagues - first in Wichita, and then in Topeka. It was in Topeka that I was introduced to AAU basketball. At the time, AAU was just winding down from its heyday for guys my age. A few years earlier the AAU was the way to go if you didn't make the NBA. Firms like Caterpillar and Marathon Oil would hire good college basketball players as managers, but then allow them to play a full basketball schedule on the AAU circuit. (As late as 1967, the AAU All-stars and the NAIA All-stars shared the Pan Am Trials championship in a round-robin tournament that included the Army All-stars and the NCAA All-stars.) I played with a team made up mostly of players who played on one of my college rivals' team – Washburn University. We had a good team and experienced some success, but I was soon transferred to St. Louis and had to start over finding a good team to play on. Fortunately for me, one of my Benedict's teammates, Jim Buford, was playing in a league in a Salvation Army college/semi-pro level league in St. Louis and asked me to join their team. Ironically, we beat a team in the league championship game that included another Benedict's teammate of mine, All-American Vince DeGreeff. After the championship game both teams went out

31

for a celebratory beer (or two) and decided to merge teams and compete on the 1975-76 AAU circuit. We had a really nice club with solid players at every position. Rich Niemann, our 7-foot center, had just been released by the Celtics, and our front line had players from St. Louis University and St. Benedict's. My teammates at guard both had played on very good Washington University (St. Louis) teams. We weren't extremely athletic, but we were smart, mentally and physically tough, played well together, and could really shoot it. The guy organizing the team got the Kutis Funeral Home brothers to sponsor us, so we went out on the road and competed against the best amateurs in the country every-other weekend. We had a blast. These guys were not only fun to play with on the court, they were also really enjoyable to be around off the court. It was the beginning of what has become a 40-year relationship – some of us still compete in state and national age-division tournaments around the country. The Funeral Home still sponsors the team in the Salvation Army League in South St. Louis, although only one of the original members is still involved. Fortunately, only one of us has died, but it won't be long before the Kutis boys are going to cash in big!

In April of 1976, our Kutis team won the National Amateur Basketball Association's (NABA) national championship in St. Paul – Minneapolis. The eight regional champions came to Minnesota for a Friday through Sunday one-and-done tourney. We won the three games by a total of six points! (It really helps when your 7-foot center shoots free throws so good that you pick him to shoot all the technical foul shots.) It was my second experience at winning a national championship, and the feeling was the

St. Louis Kutis – 1976 NABA National Champions

same as the first, only this time I played 30 minutes a game. Interestingly, we were "coached" by a really nice man named Charlie Weber. Charlie normally handled the substitutions, but his main job was to keep the score book on the bench and hand out the gum before the game. We actually coached ourselves. It wasn't hard, because we all shared the same philosophy and were all unselfish. We loved playing defense and executing on offense. We were very good at getting the ball off the board and fast-breaking, but also had the discipline to pull the ball out and run you through about a thousand screens in the half court set when we didn't score off of our break. It was very similar to the way we played at St. Benedict's, and I used that model when I became a college coach later in life.

My last couple of years of playing in St. Louis was during the time I became a single parent. I had tried to take the boys (Alex and Scott) with me as much as possible when I was married, but it was no longer an option once I was separated and then later divorced. It was great to have the kids along. It gave me a good excuse for not hitting the bars after road games.

Home games were different – it was a tradition after the Thursday night Salvation Army league games to go to our favorite local bar and grab some sandwiches and some pitchers and tell lies about how good we thought we played that night. While we'd be at the table having a good time, Alex, Scott, and my teammates' kids would be over at the nickel machine trying to win the jackpot. (The nickel machine looked like a pinball machine, but it had different slots for nickels to fall into – I'm not sure how it worked, but periodically the kids would somehow win and carry over their pot of gold to the table.) One night when they won Scott wanted to use some of the money to play the jukebox, so we said he could. He went over and put some money in the juke box, and "Begin the Beguine" came on. (This was an old "big band" era hit that no one would ever play, but we tagged Scott – at 5 years old – as having this as his favorite song.) From then on, Scott never asked to play the jukebox again!

Validating The "Right Way To Play"

"A rose is a rose is a rose." (Gertrude Stein, American novelist, poet, playwright, and art collector)

In 1978 I had been transferred by Bell back to Topeka but was still playing for Kutis whenever I could. We played in a great AAU tournament down in Ponca City, Oklahoma, that first year I was away from St. Louis. Also playing in that tournament was a team from Topeka, Hughes Conoco.

Hughes had a player from Emporia State University, Dale Cushinberry, playing for them. I had played against Dale for three years while he was an All-American at Emporia State. Hughes had brought in some "ringers" from K-

Legacy teammates at my wedding, including "Cush" standing at far left.

State and KU, and Dale, being in his 30's, wasn't getting to play too much with Hughes. He and I ran into each other at breakfast one morning at McDonald's and got to talking about how we enjoyed playing with certain people. We had a mutual respect for each other's game, and decided to form a new team in Topeka, since I couldn't travel as much with Kutis and he wasn't valued any more by Hughes. So, the next year we put together the Douglas Construction AAU team in Topeka. Somehow, I was chosen to be the player-coach, which was the start to my coaching adult level basketball. (Back in Topeka I was now coaching Alex's 3rd and 4th grade teams and would continue coaching his and Scott's teams all the way through high school summer leagues. Interestingly, even at that level you learn what motivates players to reach their potential – some need a pat on the back, and some need, as my dad used to say to us, a "swift kick in the seat of the pants"!) I remember that first year with Douglas going to a prayer group meeting and praying that I would make the right decisions concerning this team. The Douglas team wasn't like the Kutis team – it was more diverse and had a few guys who had a little bit bigger ego than the Kutis guys. Overall, though, everyone wanted to win and was willing to play hard, and "Cush" was simply a great player (and mentor to the younger players) who refused to lose. We ended the first year 26-3 and lost in the AAU Regional Tournament in Albuquerque.

I kept playing and coaching AAU ball until I was 38. I just couldn't guard anymore at that level and had to settle for playing (and coaching) in age-division tournaments. I had already played on an all-star team from Oklahoma that won the over-30 AAU national title in Salt Lake City (interestingly, Terry Stotts, the Portland Trail Blazers coach, was on that team), but now it was time to consider putting together an over-35 group for the AAU Nationals in Boca-Raton, Florida. I took a team from Topeka consisting of guys from Topeka and KC who had played for and against Douglas Construction and were now over 35. We won the championship that first year down in Florida. The following year I had been transferred back to St. Louis, so I travelled with the Kutis team as the player-coach and competed

St. Louis Reebok Over-40 AAU National Champions

in the
over-40 tournament. We got beat, mainly because we didn't have much of an inside game, since Niemann couldn't go. (We did beat a Florida team with

Artis Gilmore on it when the three of us guards combined for 97 points – we were so hot that we melted the contacts right out of their eyes!) The next year Artis brought two 6-10 guys with him and they kicked our butts – so the following year we did some recruiting of our own. We added Randy Noll, a 6-10 forward who played at Kentucky before transferring to Marshall and played with Mike D'Antoni when they were in the top 10 in the country. After college, even though he was drafted by the NBA, he decided to go to Europe where he played for quite a few years. We also added 6-7 forward/post John Brown, the former Missouri All-American and first round draft pick who had started for the Hawks and then went to Europe to complete his career after 7 years in the NBA. Both Randy and John fit in perfectly with the Kutis way of playing the game – and both were terrific players. Our opening round game was once again against Artis, whom John had played against often in the NBA, and who had actually been a teammate in John's only year with the Chicago Bulls. Prior to our game, we had a coach's meeting at the hotel and, since we had not played together previously, we went around the room and simply stated what we thought our individual strengths were. When we got to John, he simply said he was just trying to fit in. After John was asked a second time and responded the same way, Randy said, "Bull**** John, we didn't ask you to join us to 'fit in' – what are you good at. You have to know John – he is very humble – but he matter-of-factly said, "I can post up anybody." That was good enough for us – we went to him the first four possessions against Artis and he hit a turnaround jumper, a baseline jumper, a short hook, and a three-pointer from the top of the key. John ended up with 34, we won by 20, and we proceeded to win the AAU over-40 national title. This experience solidified my coaching belief that a player must know what his role is in order to maximize his benefit to the team.

Since that time, our St. Louis Kutis team (or the core of those teams) has won other national titles at the over-40, 45, 50, 55, 60 and 65 levels, as well as the previously mentioned Nike World Championship at the over-45 level. I had the privilege of being the player-coach on those teams, which allowed me the opportunity to be a candidate for the head coaching job at Benedictine when it was offered to me in 1998. It was a big risk for Benedictine, but without this experience, I would never have been considered for such a position.

So, You Want to Be a Coach ... Lesson #2:

If you have a "Dream Job" in mind, get your feet wet early, even if it means doing it for free.

Chapter 3: The Dream Job

"Choose a job you love, and you will never have to work a day in your life." (Confucius, 6th century B.C. Chinese Philosopher)

A s I had previously mentioned, we could not announce my taking the head coaching position at BC until 90 days prior to my birthday, due to the rules at SW Bell concerning eligibility for a discounted pension. (You had to reach your 50th birthday and have at least 25 years of service to qualify. If you declared more than 90 days prior to your 50th birthday, Bell could terminate your employment and you would not qualify for the pension. Not that they would necessarily do that, but I didn't want to take any chances.) So, President Carey at BC agreed not to make the coaching position announcement until May 21st or so. He called a press conference and held it at the new student union/basketball gymnasium building on May 21, and pretty much shocked everyone when he announced my appointment.

The Press Conference

"It's not what you achieve, it's what you overcome. That's what defines your career." (Carlton Fisk, Boston Red Sox Hall of Fame catcher)

There were a couple of newspapers at the press conference and the St. Joseph, MO TV station, as well as quite a few of the loyal fans from Atchison. (**See Exhibit 1**, an article written by the Sports Editor of the St. Joseph News-Press. Little did I know that he was somewhat of a prophet.) Most of the administration and fans knew me already, due to my continued relationship with the college and my having been a member of the '67 national championship team. (There is a song by Miranda Lambert called "Everyone Dies Famous in a Small Town", and that is so true. We had won the championship 31 years earlier, and I still couldn't walk down Commercial Street in Atchison without a number of people stopping me to say hello and to tell me that they were at that championship game in KC that night in 1967.)

I remember how happy I was that day when Dr. Carey said, "I'd like to introduce our new men's head basketball coach, Joe Brickner." I was

BC President Dan Carey handing mic to new head coach

absolutely convinced that I could turn that program around, and I couldn't wait to get started. I'm sure that I raised a few eyebrows when I told the group that my goal was to bring home another national championship to BC. I did not talk about conference championships or the like – I went straight to the top. I'm sure the opposing coaches in the league had a good laugh when they read the press release, and probably vowed to themselves to show this amateur a thing or two about college basketball that following season. I know it was a bold statement, but I had to change the mindset not only of the players, but also of the administration and fans. I had to give them new hope. Men's basketball had lost for so many years that people just expected it. That had to change.

Getting Started

"What you have become is the price you paid to get what you used to want."
(Mignon McLaughlin, American journalist and author)

I remember watching a movie where I think it was Robert Redford who is running for the US Senate. He was a huge underdog, but, as movies famously do, he miraculously won. The movie ended with him looking at his staff after the results were in and saying, "Now what do we do?"

Wife Kitty made Coach smile!

For me, when it was announced that I had been hired as Benedictine College's next head men's basketball coach, it wasn't quite that bad, but I must admit that I had to ponder "Where should I start?" As you can imagine, I heard from many friends, alumni, and basketball acquaintances when the announcement was made. One that was critical, in my mind, was Coach Tom Colwell. I don't remember if he contacted me or I contacted him, but he was one of the first ones I wanted to talk to about coaching. As mentioned earlier, Coach Colwell was the assistant coach at St. Benedict's when we won the National Championship in 1967. He was the X and O's guy. He ran most of our practices. Like many people in multiple professions, I thought it wise to model my basketball program after other successful programs. Coach had been very successful as an assistant and later as head coach at St. Benedict's, but also highly respected as a head coach at a couple of KC high schools.

Coach and I always had a close relationship, and to say he was enthusiastic about helping me get off to a good start as a college coach would be an understatement. He invited me to come to his house in Kansas City as soon as I relocated from St. Louis, and he told me he'd share everything he had with me. He wasn't kidding.

After I relocated from St. Louis, I arranged to go to Coach's and his wonderful wife Kitty's home for an evening of Basketball 101. He showed me how he organized practices and prepared for games. He literally gave me his playbook, which contained multiple offenses, defenses, and plays for special situations. (Coach, at this time, was still teaching at a public high school, but he had retired from head coaching. He volunteered as an assistant coach at a local Catholic High School, so his need for his playbook was no longer important.) I learned so much that evening. My memory of our college practices was pretty good, but learning how to progress from the first day of practice to the first game and then through a full season was very helpful. Plus, from my AAU and coaching days, I knew how to address certain special situations, but not necessarily all of them. He helped me with this also.

His playbook contained not only offensive patterns and defensive assignments, but also practice drills to be used to build from one-on-one all the way to five-on-five scenarios.

It was truly a beneficial evening spent at the Colwell's, but probably most important to me wasn't the X's and O's - it was the realization that Coach and Kitty were there for me, regardless of what I needed. Their encouragement and support were so reassuring, and I knew I could call on them whenever I needed. And there were a number of times in my first couple of years that I did just that.

Being "Spoon-fed"

"He who walks with wise men will be wise, but the companion of fools will suffer harm." (Proverbs 13:20)

Another source for me starting out was Coach Charlie Spoonhour, who at the time was St. Louis University's head men's basketball coach. I called and made an appointment to visit with Coach Spoon in his office on SLU's campus. Talk about a gracious person - he was so open and informative.

We spent about 90 minutes talking about his "philosophy" and how he was able to convey that philosophy in a way that his players bought into it. Coach Spoon was a legend in Missouri. (In Missouri they called his style "Spoon ball.") He had found success in Missouri at the high school, junior college, and major college levels. He became known nationally while at Southwest Missouri State, where he made them a mid-major power that the big schools did not want to have to play in the early rounds of the NCAA tournament. I was so fortunate to have had the opportunity to pick his brain. We didn't spend hardly any time on X's and O's. Instead Coach Spoon talked about mental and physical

Coach Spoon

toughness, and how that has been a cornerstone of his programs. Spoon's teams were always very good defensive teams, so I naturally asked him how he taught defense and what his main man-to-man principles were. He gave me a good overview of his system but emphasized that there is not one "best" system. He explained there are number of different systems that could be effective but the key to success is execution. And reflecting back on my experience as a player on successful teams at all levels, he was spot-on. My challenge, I knew, was to get "buy in" from my players and staff that our system would work, and it would be worth the dedicated effort that it would take to learn and become good at our system at both ends of the court.

The visit with Coach Spoonhour was both beneficial and enjoyable. He was a very personable and gracious person, extremely comfortable in his own skin. He was a huge Cardinal baseball fan. He also knew quite a few of my AAU and college teammates from his days as a high school coach. I treasure the time I had with him and took his advice to heart. Unfortunately, Spoon passed away in 2012 – but I bet his lifelong dream of playing second base for the Cardinals has been realized in Heaven!!

OJT – On the Job Training

"Tell me and I forget, teach me and I may remember, involve me and I learn."
(Benjamin Franklin, statesman and inventor)

If I have one regret, it's that I never got an opportunity to be an assistant to a successful college coach. To be able to "shadow" a Larry Brown or a Bill Self, or at the small college-level someone like Don Meyer, for a year or two would have been invaluable to me. "Game management "is not something that comes naturally to most coaches, in my opinion. As a head coach, or even as an assistant, you can't observe the action the same way a fan does. There are so many things to consider - overall game strategy, quality of execution, strategic adjustments, foul situation, health and skill level of players, the way the game is being officiated, etc., etc. I will admit that I was blessed to be able to work with three assistant coaches in my first few years who had head coaching experience. Unfortunately, I only had $6000 allocated by the college to pay an assistant, so these three outstanding coaches had to have other full-time jobs in order to make a living. Chic Downing, a former college teammate of mine and an All-American who was drafted by the New York Knicks, bailed me out my first year when the previous year's assistant coach quit just one week before practice started. Coach Downing had been a head high school coach in Atchison and won 4 state championships. Mike Martin, who helped me for a couple of years after Chic's health caused him to have to give up coaching, was a former head coach at Joliet Juco in Joliet IL, and was a very demanding coach who pushed the kids hard. Joe Huber was a volunteer for part of three seasons. Coach Huber had been a very successful Indiana high school head coach and an assistant at Bowling Green State University and at the University of Delaware. I learned a ton from these great coaches, but it would still have been beneficial to observe from close-range the adjustments a Larry Brown would make as a game progressed, and then be able to ask him after the game why he did what he did when he did it. For me I had to learn that on the fly. Not that I didn't experience some of this as a player and a player/coach, especially due to the fact that I always played the point guard position. From that position you get the best perspective of what a coach is facing. But it's still different. As an example, to be able to draw up a play during a timeout based on what you personally observed during the game is not always a simple matter. Regardless of how well you prepare for a team, you can't practice for all situations. You must be able to be creative sometimes. The first time I remember successfully doing that was in my second year in a game against Park University on a neutral court in a tournament up in Nebraska. Park, a NAIA Division 1 team, was very athletic and had been pressing us man-to-man full court the entire game. Although we had fewer scholarships than Park, we were in a battle with them the whole game. They tied the game with about five seconds left in regulation. There are plays designed for when you need to go the full length of the court and score with 5 seconds or less in a period, and we practiced one of them usually the day before a game. In this case, though, since Park had been in a full-court denial man-to-man press the whole game, that play did not fit the situation. I was pretty sure that they would keep the press on after our time out. We had been using a two-man stack at about the free throw line to break their press. In this set the man at the free throw line would turn and set a back pick on the guard at the top of the key, and then roll to the ball hoping to shed his defender on the switch by the defense. He would hopefully be open to receive the inbounds pass. If he wasn't open, our two big guys, who lined up at half-court on opposite side lines, would break to the ball for the inbounds pass. Park had been guarding our two big guys with two of their big guys, but they guarded our two guards with their three remaining players. (They did not put a man on the ball guarding the in-bounder.) In the huddle I told our big guys to not wait to break toward the ball like they normally would - instead they would break as soon as our first guard turned to go set his pick on our second guard at the top of the key. I then instructed the first guard, Poochie Earl, who was my first recruit, to fake setting the pick and just blow by the second guard and sprint to our end of the court. The in-bounder, a freshman named Patrick McGowan, my first high school recruit, was to throw a baseball pass over the top to a streaking Poochie. Hopefully, Park's three guards would anticipate the pick and switch like they normally had been doing. Also, their big men would follow our two big men up towards the ball as they have been doing all night. This would clear out the whole back side for Poochie. I still remember the ref handing the ball to Pat, Poochie turning to supposedly set the pick, and our two big guys breaking toward the in-bounder, and then Poochie flying by the defender like a wide receiver going long. Pat lofted a perfect pass to Poochie, who caught it in stride. Unfortunately, as he

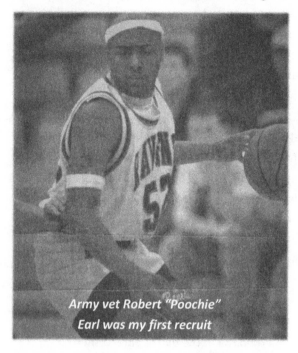

Army vet Robert "Poochie"
Earl was my first recruit

went up for the game-winning layup, one of their defenders fouled him from behind, forcing Poochie to miss the lay-up. So now there are two seconds on the clock and Poochie is shooting two free throws. Even though Poochie had the best hands on the team to catch a long pass, and he was a strong finisher at the basket, he was one of our poorest free throw shooters at around 50%. With the game on the line, Poochie missed his first free throw. With all of us praying on the

sidelines, Poochie lined up his second shot, and just like in Hoosiers, he rattled in the second shot and we won the game by a point! It was a satisfying win beating a bigger school, and it was personally satisfying knowing the kids executed a play perfectly that we had never practiced.

As time went on and I studied more training films of the top coaches and what to do in special situations, we would use plays that we had practiced most of the time. Still, there were situations where our standard plays didn't fit, and you had to improvise. Later in my career, when John Peer, a former player and grad assistant for me, had some experience under his belt, I'd simply say to John, "John, if this game comes down to the last possession and we have to score, we'll have our point guard call time-out near our sideline in the front of our bench. We'll need to have a play set up to score rather quickly from a sideline inbounds pass." I'd give him similar type parameters, based on the game situation, and he would stop watching the game and either use one of our set plays I kept in a binder next to my chair or draw one up he had seen on TV. (He loved watching college and pro coaches draw up special situation plays, and would copy them down for us to use, if necessary.) He would draw up the play on a clipboard, I'd call a timeout, and he'd conduct the huddle showing each player what to do. More often than not, the plays worked.

Now I know many fans and probably the school's president and athletic administration thought this was bizarre behavior on my part, allowing the assistant to conduct such a huddle with the game on the line. But to me, it made sense. Just like in business, when you have a problem, you put a top specialist on it to resolve. I trusted John - he had been with me since his freshman year and knew how I thought. He was young, but he had a good coaching mind. Plus, he loved drawing up plays that worked. So why not let him draw up a play and explain it to our players and let me continue to coach the game until his play was needed. In my mind, the only reason not to do this was my ego. In other words, there was no good reason not to do it.

So, You Want to Be a Coach ... Lesson #3:
Don't hesitate to ask for help and guidance from experts in the "Dream" field you are pursuing, even if you don't personally know the expert.

Chapter 4: Call Me "Coach"

"Life is like a dogsled team. If you ain't the lead dog, the scenery never changes." (Lewis Gizzard, American writer and humorist)

I remember how strange it felt the first month or two when I was referred to as "Coach" instead of "Joe" or on occasion "Mr. Brickner." Not from the kids, mind you, but from administrators and other coaches. In business I always stressed to those who worked in my organization as well as other coordinates of mine to call me by my first name. I personally felt that we were and still are all equal in the eyes of God, and that having someone refer to me differently than by my first name made it appear that in some way I was superior to them. I never felt superior to anyone – I just happened to have a job that gave me more authority than some others. But all of us had a job, and each of us tried to do that job as best that we were able. Therefore, my respect for the janitor was at the same level as my respect for the CEO. My expectations were that those who I worked with felt the same way, and gave me respect not because of my title, but rather because of my work ethic, honesty, and a true care for their well-being. So being addressed by a title by those with whom I came into contact after I was hired as the head men's basketball coach took a little time to get used to for me. Also, I felt like I did not deserve to be called "Coach", since I hadn't earned my stripes at the college level yet. But "Coach" it was, and I quickly adjusted to responding when someone would holler "Hey Coach"!

I loved coaching. Unfortunately, about 80% of my time was spent doing things other than coaching – but that 20% was wonderful. Using the gym as a classroom to convey knowledge and strategies/plans to young men was everything I dreamed it would be. There is no better feeling than when you show someone how to do something properly, and then they learn to do it and do it consistently. The ultimate is when they transfer this knowledge/skill from the practice floor to the game floor. I had experienced this myself as a player, but it went to another level for me when I was able to teach someone something that helped them be successful. Teachers experience this every day in the classroom, and frankly, coaches are teachers who use a gym for a classroom rather than a 20' x 30' room.

Teaching the Basics

"If you miss the first buttonhole, you will not succeed in buttoning up your coat." (Johann von Goethe, German poet, playwright, novelist, scientist, statesman, theatre director, critic, and amateur artist)

I was somewhat surprised when I got to BC at how much I needed to teach in the way of fundamentals. I am not criticizing my predecessor – I wasn't at any of his practices, so I do not know what or how he taught. I do know that the way I learned to play the game was foreign to the players I had my first year at the helm. Something as simple as stopping at the free throw line when you are the middleman leading the 3 on 2 fast break was a concept that was new to the team and had to be drilled consistently before they began to use this technique in game situations. And it took all season to get this ingrained in them – shoot, as late as the playoff semifinals we were still pulling players off the court if they failed to do this in a game.

> I remember in the second half of our league's semi-final playoff game at William Jewell, my assistant coach, Chic Downing, saw a 3 on 2 go awry because our guard did not stop at the free throw line. He immediately grabbed our top sub and had him check in for the guard who made the mistake. Upon coming off the floor, the guard knew what he had done and knew he was about to get a lecture. He did, and 30 seconds later he checked back into the game. Now this was a senior guard to boot playing in what ended up being his last game. The message was sent not only to the senior guard, but everyone on the team – play the way we practice, or you won't play. (I know some of you are thinking, "The assistant coach made this substitution? You let your assistant do this?" The answer is yes – he and I were on the same page, and he had the authority to do exactly what he did. Heck, the man won four state championships as a high school coach and was state runner-up three other years – he knew what he was doing, and I trusted him to do the right thing.)

Strengths

"The most difficult thing in life is to know thyself." (Thales, Pre-Socratic philosopher, mathematician and astronomer)

In my opinion, one of my biggest strengths is organizational skills, and I put them to use every day at practice. We had a minute-by-minute schedule for our 2 ½ hour practices. (**See Exhibit 2.** In my later years, we cut the practices back to no more than two hours per day.) We used the game clock to time every segment of the practice schedule – even the time for them to get a drink of water. Every practice was planned in detail and had drills which had a specific purpose. If it was pre-season, each drill built on the previous day's drills to move our team closer to being game-ready for our first game of the season. If it was a practice after the season started, each drill prepared us for what we wanted to do in our next game, corrected errors that were made in our previous game, or built on something we planned to implement later in the season. Even our conditioning drills had a purpose over and above getting us into game condition.

One drill we used was the "minute drill." Most kids hated it, for you had to run the length of the court 10 times in a minute or less. If anyone on your "line" didn't make it in one minute, all players in that line had to run it again and make the time. It is a great conditioning drill, but we added another element to it. I forced every player running to do so with a ball, dribbling while they ran without turning the ball over. They had to use their right hand to dribble down the court, and their left hand to dribble back. Now this was no big deal for our guards, but some of our forwards and centers really had a hard time handling the ball (especially with their off-hand) and still making the time. It's amazing, though, at how quickly they learn the skill when faced with having to run another minute run if they fail to make the time or have a turnover dribbling. Why would I do that? For the guards, they have to be able to push the ball up the court as fast as they can at times in games, and this prepared them for that situation. For the bigs, it gave them confidence in a game that if they had to handle the ball in the open court, they could do it without turning it over. It irritated me that coaches always told their big kids that they couldn't handle the ball in the open court. Well, if you don't practice it, that is true. But why not incorporate a ball handling drill into a conditioning drill and get the best of both worlds? Now don't misunderstand me. If our big got the ball in the open court and there was a guard open and, on the move, the big was to pass him the ball and then sprint down an open lane to try to get an easy basket. However, if there was no guard open and the big could advance the ball without being guarded closely, he was expected to do that. It helped create 4 on 3 and 3 on 2 situations - plus it forced the defense to adjust and not be given time to "set up."

Another strength I have, and used similarly to the way I managed in business, is the ability to delegate responsibility and authority. From that business background came my belief that when you have people working for you who are very good at a certain task, you allow them to use that skill to its highest potential. I followed that creed from Day 1 as a Coach. If I had an assistant who was excellent at teaching a big man how to use offensive moves in the post, I would allow that coach to work with our big men while I took our perimeter players.

A good example of this was my assistant Coach Peer's innate ability, as I mentioned earlier, to draw up a play during a time-out, even at a young age. He was a student of the game and watched college and pro games on TV all the time. (I didn't have time to watch TV.) He would see a play that would work in a certain situation and write it down for future reference. He would show it to me, and we'd discuss its possible use for us in certain situations. Subsequently during our games, if the opportunity presented itself, I would allow him to draw up the play and cover it with the team in the huddle. Quite often the plays would be successful. Interestingly, a by-product of this delegation of authority was a situation whereby, from some players' perspective, Coach Peer was the brains of the outfit, and I was simply a figurehead. It wasn't a case of where I was unable to draw up a play – most who have played or studied the game could do that – it was a case where Coach Peer, as the assistant coach, would have time while a game was going on to analyze the situation from his second seat on the bench and consider what may or may not work from our catalog of plays. He would even pre-draw it so that we

Coach Peer on right with Basketball Chaplain Fr. Hugh Keefer

could cover the responsibilities of each player during a 30 second time-out, if necessary. Because of the fact that the players had never been exposed to "delegation of authority", some interpreted it such that Coach Peer was more qualified than I was to be the head coach. I believe that some players lost respect for me because of that. However, I did not change what I was doing. After I started to realize the reaction of some team members, I told them in a team meeting why I did what I did in those situations.

I had one player in particular who was very fond of Coach Peer, and vice-versa. In order to show him that I actually could draw up a play that could work, I decided to do just that in our last scrimmage game of his senior year. We trailed a team by one point with about 6 seconds to go in the game. We had the ball out on the side after I had called a time out. During the time-out I drew up a play that I had used a number of times in AAU ball. It was a baseline double pick play for our best shooter, who happened to be this very senior. However, instead of passing to the shooter, one of the men setting the double pick would slip to basket immediately after setting the pick. Sure enough, he was wide open, we got him the ball, and he scored a layup at the buzzer. Our kids went nuts, even though it was just a scrimmage. They were all impressed with the play, but probably even more so because I drew it up. I accepted their congratulations in the locker room, but quickly moved on to talk about the good things we did and the things we still needed to work on. I have to admit that it did feel good to call a play that won the game, but when the season started, Coach Peer was back in the position of drawing up plays prior to time-outs – because he was really good at it.

The System

"If you board the wrong train, it is no use running along the corridor in the other direction." (Dietrich Bonhoeffer, German pastor, theologian, anti-Nazi dissident)

One of the biggest challenges I faced most years was to adjust our "system" to the talent and skill level of the new team. Almost all of our players stayed for all four years, which in many cases meant that we had to replace key starters every year due to graduation. The "next generation" of Ravens, including the new recruits, may or may not have had the skill sets of those who played the year before. Unfortunately, we could not be extremely selective on signing kids who had the skill sets to match our offensive and defensive "systems." We simply had to sign the best talented kids we were able to sign and who fit with the academic and social culture of Benedictine. This caused us to have to re-evaluate just what offense and what defense best matched our team's attributes. Most years we had to change what offense we ran and some years even our defense had to change. Therefore, I spent most summers researching and learning offenses or defenses that best fit our next season's team. We did have a few offensive plays (quick hitters) that we used year in and year out, but as far as an overall strategy, it had to change with the personnel we had available.

(As an example of a quick hitter we used practically every year, we had a play we called "High." It was a 3-out, 2-in set that started with our best post-up player moving from one of the blocks to the free throw line as a decoy. We would fake a pass from the wing to him, and then he'd go set a down pick on the other "big" who had moved from the other low block to the middle of the lane right in front of the rim. The guy getting a pick would break to the free throw line and receive a pass from the wing, while simultaneously the picker would "seal" his man as deeply as possible in front of the rim. The player with the ball at the free throw line would then pass down to the player posted in the paint, who could then go either direction with his post move to score. If the defense tried to "double down", then the player at the free throw line had a wide open 15-footer. That play worked so often for us that we kept it in our arsenal each year.)

Changing offensive or defensive tactics/plays meant redesigning pre-season practices each year to meet the needs of teaching the new offense/defense. After about our third year, we pretty much solidified the fundamental half-court man-to-man defense, so most years we did not have to change pre-season drills for that. But there were still years where we'd run a full court 1-2-1-1 press, or a 2-2-1 zone press, or even one year we ran a pretty good 1-3-1 half court press. It all depended upon our roster.

One year I had 10 equally talented players and ran a 5-in, 5-out substitution pattern in games. One team ran an up-tempo offense and a full court man-to-man pressure defense, while the other group ran a very patterned offensive set and a match up half-court zone. That year took a lot of planning to maximize our practice time due to the divergent offenses and defenses that we ran.

I would have preferred to have one system on offense and one on defense and simply recruit kids who fit the system, like the Duke's, North Carolina's and Kansas's do. I think that type of consistency provides an advantage for those

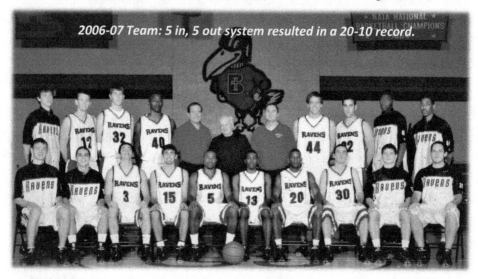

2006-07 Team: 5 in, 5 out system resulted in a 20-10 record.

teams – plus some kids go to those schools because the type of system the school plays best fits that player's skills/desires. Maybe after the scholarship levels were raised at our school, we could have accomplished this, since we could have been more selective on whom we recruited. But during my tenure, it simply wasn't an option, in my opinion.

I will admit, though, that I enjoyed searching for the best match each summer for the team that we had assembled for the following fall. My last year may have been my favorite for this phenomenon. Thanks to a recommendation from the outstanding women's coach at BC, Chad Folsom, we ran Coach John Calipari's "Dribble-Drive" offense in 2009-10. At a small school like BC, men's and women's coaches become very familiar with the talent/skill levels and attributes of each other's teams. Because of limited gym time, weight room time, etc., close coordination is required between the two programs. So sharing ideas among coaches, at least at BC, was not unusual. And since Brad and I had a great relationship, neither he nor I would hesitate to point out something we noticed that might be of benefit to the other coach. In this particular case, Chad knew what we had coming back and what we had recruited for 2009-10, and suggested I look at the Dribble-Drive offense as an option for the upcoming season. He gave me a couple of training films on how to run the offense and some drills that would help teach the principles of the offense. I studied them that summer and shared them with my assistant coach, John Peer. We decided that it was a good

2009-10 Raven basketball teams. Coach Folsom is next to me without the tie. (Ready for practice)

match for us and implemented it the following season.

Let me take a minute to explain, briefly, the offense. It is a 4 out, 1 in set where the four perimeter players play outside of the three-point line, and the post player plays on the deep short baseline (behind the backboard) opposite the ball. The whole theory is to put maximum pressure on the ball defender by driving hard to the basket each time you receive a pass on the perimeter. (If you can't immediately drive, you pass to the next perimeter position and make a hard basket cut looking for a return pass.) When you drive, your goal is to get by your defender and force the post defender to make a decision – does he leave his man and try to keep you from scoring a layup, or does he stay with his own man? Obviously, if he stays with his own man, you go strong to the hoop and score. If he comes to get you, you simply pass the ball up near the rim where your post teammate catches and finishes. (Think back to the number of times you have seen Coach Calipari's post players catch and dunk a lob from a driving perimeter player.) Now in order to run this offense you need four perimeter players who can handle the basketball and score off the dribble as well as shoot the three for when people back off of them or try to help on a driver.

Chad's insight was spot-on. Our kids picked up the offense quickly and we really got good at it. We beat two of the three NCAA schools we played that year in regular season games (losing by a basket to the one that beat us) and were 13-4 and ranked 13th in the country in NAIA Division 1 in late January. Now our defense was good (our 6-10 center was leading the country in blocked shots and rebounding), but it was the offense that made us go. People really had a hard time guarding us due to our perimeter quickness and shooting ability. Unfortunately, our 6-10 center's knees gave out in our 18th game, our 6'6" leading scorer contracted a virus and had no energy from about our 19th game on, his backup had the same virus, and the center's back-up sprained his ankle so badly that he missed our last four games. Without a front line on defense, we simply couldn't compete and ended up with a 16-14 record. It was too bad – these kids worked hard, loved what they were doing on the court, and bought in to the system. Had they stayed healthy, they would have been rewarded with a trip to the national tournament, in my opinion.

Keeping Them Sane

"A man can stand almost anything except a succession of ordinary days."
(Johann von Goethe, German poet, playwright, novelist, scientist, statesman, theatre director, critic, and amateur artist)

One of the most trying times for a small college coach is during the Christmas holidays, especially if your school is located in a small rural town. You not only had to deal with the kids being out of their normal school routine, eating poorly, sleeping too little or too much, getting sick, etc., you had to deal with their boredom. Other than practice, the kids simply did not have anything to do. I always tried to raise enough money so that we could go somewhere, preferably warm, for a classic or a tournament during Christmas break. Even with that, you could only afford to be on the road for 4 or 5 days at the most. (In a later chapter I talk about the infamous Christmas break trip to Ohio to play Findlay University and a couple of other schools. It was a traveler's nightmare, and it was the one of the few times we did not go south or west for a holiday trip.) If you gave them a week off for Christmas, that meant you had them on campus for about 4 weeks with no students there.

One year, in order to save on expenses, I gave the team three weeks off at Christmas. I told them to be sure to get to a gym and workout, because the first practice back we were going to do at least 5 minute-runs to start practice. I had scheduled the team to play in a Classic at Grand Canyon University in Phoenix, so the players reported in the day before our first game. We practiced at a local Phoenix high school, and true to my word, after warming up, I lined up the kids for the minute-runs. After the second minute run I had more than half the team bent over trash bins puking their guts out. Needless to say, we lost both games in that Classic, and I never again gave them more than five or six days off at Christmas.

The good thing about the holidays, though, was that it was a great opportunity to make adjustments based upon first semester results. We used to have two-a-day practices most of the time – one practice designed to put in new things, and one to get them ready for the next game.

Unplanned Situations

"Life consists of not holding good cards, but in playing those you do hold well." (Josh Billings, the pen name of 19th-century American humorist Henry Wheeler Shaw.)

Although our practices were well scripted, there were times when things didn't go as planned.

During one practice in my second last year of coaching I had something happen that probably hasn't happened to many college coaches. I had a 7-foot kid who transferred in from an NCAA D2 school in August. He was the brother of a former 4-year player of ours, came from a great family, and was a really good kid. However, he was an introvert and didn't really know anyone on campus when he arrived. He turned 22 years old in September, and normally a 22-year-old transfer could live off-campus. However, since he was not 22 in August when he arrived, and he had lived on campus at his previous school, BC had a rule that he had to stay in a dorm on campus his junior year unless he had won the "off-campus lottery" for all upper-classmen the previous April. (Since he wasn't a BC student in April, there was no way for him to qualify.) I did everything I could to petition the VP – Dean of Students to allow him to move in with another very introverted transfer, who needed a roommate, in a house that was directly across the street from our campus, but to no avail. Since they were out of rooms in the normal junior dorms, they assigned him to the worst dorm on campus (over 100-year-old St. Joe Hall with its small single rooms in a depressingly old building) with 25 other poor souls. So now he is living in a dorm by himself with people he doesn't know. He really disliked the food service on campus and wasn't all that fired up about his classes. He simply was not a happy student/athlete, but he didn't complain. He looked forward to practices and games, but nothing else was working for him. He finally broke one day after the students returned from Christmas break. We were doing some conditioning work in the middle of one of our practices, the minute runs I mentioned earlier, and he was unable to make the required 10 dribbling sprints in a minute. He had failed 2 times in a row, and the guys having to run with him were getting upset with him. On the third attempt, it was obvious that he wasn't going to make it again, so as he approached the finish line, he kept right on running out the door and down the hallway! I was standing on the sideline and couldn't see down the hallway, so I simply waited 10 seconds or so expecting him to come back for try number four. When he didn't come back in, I moved to a position where I could see down the hall, expecting to see him bent over with his hands on his knees. Nope! There was no one in the hallway. I then asked one of the players to go out to try to find where he went, but they returned and said they couldn't find him. The kid apparently ran out of the gym, out of the building, and back to his dorm. You can imagine how astonished all of us were seeing him vanish down the hallway. After we gathered ourselves somewhat, we went ahead and finished practice not knowing what happened to this young man!

As a sidebar conversation to this story, it shows that a coach can't be just a coach. There are times when you must be a psychologist, a father, an advisor, or even just a listener. In the 7-footer's case, when I contacted him, he told me how miserable he was. (He had just scored 17 points for us in the previous game against one of the top two teams in the conference, so I thought he would have been on a high. Wrong.) As part of the conversation, he said he thought he should just drop out and go home. Since second semester had begun, I encouraged him not to do that because it could negatively affect his academic progress. As we delved deeper into his feelings, I asked him if he felt like he had to play basketball simply because he was so tall. He said he liked basketball, but yes, he was always expected to play because of his height. I then asked him if he could do anything at this point, what would it be? He said he would transfer to the college where his friends go to school and just be a student. I then encouraged him to call his parents, talk it over with them, and then make a decision as to what to do next. I did recommend at least staying out the year – with or without basketball – so that he could transfer with good grades and enough hours to be a senior. I told him if he did decide to stay, he could continue to be on the team or not play, whichever he felt was best for himself.

To be frank, I was really worried about the big kid. He was really depressed, and depression can do strange things to people. I had to go against my instinct and not contact him while he was trying to decide what to do. That was hard, for if he had done something crazy, I would have beat myself to a pulp for not intervening. The good news is that he did have a conversation with his parents and decided he wanted to return to the team. When he contacted me, I was both relieved and glad that he made the decision he made. My gladness had nothing to do with basketball, and everything to do with this kid's mental state of mind. I thought that if he was willing to go in front of the team and apologize for his behavior and ask them if they would take him back, it was a huge step in the right direction. He did just that, and not surprisingly, the team welcomed him back. Now understand that he was not a great player – he was pretty good on offense and pretty bad on defense. So the team taking him back was not because of basketball, but because they felt he deserved another chance. That really pleased me, and I think it was a life lesson for all involved. He then rejoined the team and practiced with us getting ready for the next game. I purposely did not play him the first half of the next game but did put him in for a few minutes during the second half. I could have held him out as punishment, but in this case, he had not been belligerent or insubordinate – he was depressed. I felt he had suffered enough, and by asking him to stand in front of teammates and apologize and ask them to allow him to return was humbling enough. He did not need to be punished further.

What are "The Fundamentals"

"If we take care of the inches, we will not have to worry about the miles."
(Hartley Coleridge, English poet, biographer, essayist, and teacher)

Another part of practice that I thoroughly enjoyed was teaching fundamentals. That probably sounds boring to you. For me it was not boring at all – it was rather exciting, especially when the player "got it." It didn't take me long, though, to realize I didn't know as much about the fundamentals of basketball as I thought I had known. When you play, you do many things automatically. Somewhere in your past someone probably taught you how to do things properly, but as a player matures, all those things come naturally. You simply don't have to think about footwork, or proper shooting techniques, etc. But try to teach someone else those fundamentals, and it's a different story, at least it was for me. Don't misunderstand me – I could show somebody how I did it, but that is not the same as teaching them, step by step, how to properly execute a movement. So, I had to go back to school, so to speak. I did that by purchasing as many training videos as I could that taught specific techniques. And I was very selective on whose video I bought. If I was looking for individual defensive techniques, I bought Dick Bennet's defensive fundamentals tapes. If I needed post moves techniques, I bought Pete Newell's training tapes. Depending upon what skill I was looking for, I found that skill's best coach, in my opinion, and studied his techniques. I learned a ton and was able to go out with confidence and teach the skill to my players. In addition, almost all of the training films would have specific drills to do to teach the technique/skill, and I would incorporate many of these drills into our practices. I didn't anticipate having to become a student of the game when I got hired, but student I did become. And I learned from the best, even if it was just a video tape version.

Bob Knight or John Wooden?

"All coaching is, is taking a player where he can't take himself." (Bill McCartney, American football player and coach and the founder of the Promise Keepers men's ministry)

As far as what type of practice coach I was, I was not a screamer – I tried to be a teacher and use positive reinforcement as my main source of motivation. Oh, there were times I would get upset and lose my temper a bit, but in almost every case it was due to lack of effort on the part of the team. And when I got mad, things were not good for my players. They knew that I wasn't going to rant and rave – I was simply going to say, "Get on the line, gentlemen"! I'd run the crap out of them, and then go back to whatever we were trying to achieve in practice and do it until I was satisfied with their performance.

One of the few times they were punished that did not entail a lack of effort was when I found out that they had a big drinking party during the Christmas break portion of our season. I asked at the beginning of practice who had participated (I already knew) and asked them to step forward. Only 2 kids stepped forward. I knew 2 of the remaining kids were not at the party, so I asked them to step forward. That left 8 kids who were there but would not 'fess up. I told the 2 kids who did not participate to go shoot some free throws, and then I had the rest of the team watch the two who admitted to being at the party run a few minute runs as punishment. Then I turned to the rest of the team and said, "We normally practice 2 ½ hours. We have two hours left for practice. I am going to work with these 4 gentlemen during that time. The rest of you will begin running the stairs loop." (We were practicing in our Old Gym, and it had stairs that led up one side of the gym and across the back of the bleachers to the other side of the gym. I had timed how long it would take to run one loop, so I knew how many I wanted them to have to run in the two-hour time period that would force them to have to really push it to make it.) "You have two hours to run 100 loops. If you don't make 100 in the two hours, you will do it again at tomorrow's practice and continue doing it until you make 100 loops in two hours." Now I was upset that they would damage their bodies by engaging in a booze party, but I was more upset that all 10 who had participated in the party had not stepped forward. I then said, "Integrity is a key virtue of being on this team, and by not having the fortitude to step up and admit you were part of the party, I am very disappointed in your behavior. So as a reminder in the future to be honest, you are going to run for two hours." And they did – and they never forgot! By the way, everyone made the 100 laps the first time.

My demeanor in games was somewhat reserved. My main concern was that we implemented what we had practiced. We had a game strategy developed for each game and drilled on it in practices leading up to each game. A few hours before every game we would have a "walk-through", reviewing on the court the specific plays that the opponent ran and how we were going to defend each play, including in-bounds plays. We'd also review any new offensive twists we had put in, if any, for that specific opponent. Come game time, I didn't feel like I had to be "coaching" every possession from the

Watching action from the sideline.

sideline. I knew from my playing days that having to pay attention to the sideline really took away from what was actually going on on the court. My coaching attitude was, "We have practiced and discussed what the opponent does and what we are going to do, so let the kids execute the game plan and not have to worry about what somebody is screaming at them from the sideline." I wanted the kids to be relaxed and confident on the court, and I was more of a cheerleader on the sideline most of the time. I used my time-outs to correct anything we saw that wasn't being executed properly, make any required adjustments, set up a specific play, or simply to give the kids a rest.

In NAIA games, there were no "Media Timeouts" like there were in NCAA games. Therefore, you may have a stretch of 8 to 10 to 12 minutes straight without a timeout on the court. The players have to be in much better physical condition than those who have a media timeout every 4 (NCAA Div.1) or 5 (NCAA Div. 2) minutes, and a coach normally needs a little deeper bench. Plus, you really have to guard the use of your time-outs as a coach in NAIA. We had four full time outs (60 seconds) and two 30-second timeouts for the game. The NCAA had one 60-second time out and four 30-second timeouts to go along with the eight (Div. 1) and six (Div. 2) media timeouts. (I believe both NAIA and NCAA have now gone to

75-second timeouts instead of 60-second timeouts, but when I am watching March Madness, I swear each media time-out {read "commercial"} is at least 2 to 3 minutes long.) I've always gotten a kick out of the TV game announcers for the NCAA games as the game gets into the last few minutes. They so often will say, "These guys are exhausted." Hell, how can you be exhausted if you have a built in 2-minute rest every four minutes, plus your coach's five timeouts and the opponent coach's five timeouts? If they are exhausted, there are not in basketball shape.

Homework/Feedback

"I think it is very important to have a feedback loop, where you are constantly thinking about what you have done and how you could be doing it better." (Elon Musk, South African-born American entrepreneur and businessman)

One of my regrets is that I did not have the time necessary after a game to thoroughly review the game film. In the later years, I delegated that to my assistant, for we also had to get ready for the next game, which meant reviewing film on our opponents. (In my early years, the assistant had a full-time job off campus and did not have time to do this. In my later years, the assistant would review the previous game and I would review film of the opponent for our next game in order to put together a game plan.) By not seeing first-hand how well we executed in the previous game, I felt I was missing a piece of information that was important for our improvement. My last two years it got better – I was able to raise the funds to buy a laptop and some specialized software that edited the game film and gave the person editing an opportunity to categorize each possession. It was great, because then the assistant could put all our offensive sets, by specific play, in one category, all our defensive sets in another, and our transition play in a third. That gave me a chance to see how consistent we were in executing, and where we needed to improve. It was also a great tool to show the players just what they did right and what they did wrong during that specific game. I wish we would have had that software 10 years earlier.

Beyond Being Coach

"We can always make a difference to someone, no matter what role we play."
(Lindsey Stirling, American violinist, singer and songwriter)

I viewed coaching probably a little differently than most coaches. I don't know if it was my age that caused this perspective or the fact that I had two sons who had experienced playing college basketball, but I looked upon the players more as sons than simply as student-athletes. (Actually, grandsons in my last few years!) I felt a responsibility to help these young men develop in ways other than basketball and academics. What I desired when these boys graduated from college was to have nurtured each one of them into a well-rounded young man leaving campus and entering the "real world."

One of the things I did in later years was to load the whole team up in the bus and drive to North Kansas City to attend the "etiquette dinner" sponsored by our Counseling Department. The attendees had to don formal wear, so the guys were in suits or sport jackets, and the gals were in dresses. The first time I took our team to this event I became very confused – we had about 20 guys attending, and I only recognized about half of them when they got on the bus. Golly they looked nice. Same goes for the gals. I had never seen these kids in anything but gym clothes and jeans. As the saying goes, they cleaned up pretty good!

The dinner was hosted by a group who taught proper table etiquette. They had a "Master of Ceremonies" who would tell the attendees what to do, how to do it, and when to do it. There were table monitors who would come around and make sure the attendees were doing things properly. They matched the guys with a gal and then taught them:

- how to pull out the chair for their "date"
- which glass of water was theirs and which was not
- which forks and spoons to use and when to use them, etc.

At first the guys did everything they could to get out of going (including using the excuse that they had to study that night), but in the end they had a ball. They not only got a chance to strut their stuff in front of some pretty good-looking young women, but they also got a delicious five-course meal instead of eating BC cafeteria food. It was a fun night, and I'm sure they impressed their future dates when they tipped their soup bowl <u>away</u> from themselves to finish up those last few drops instead of picking up the bowl and slurping up the soup as if it were in a glass!

Not all "social education" was formal. The second year I was at BC we played in a classic in Florida over Christmas break. For a number of players, it was the first time they would travel on a plane. This reoccurred again for a new group of players when we flew to Phoenix or San Diego for Christmas games. Even when we drove to Christmas tournaments, they were exposed to new situations.

One year we played in a tournament at St. Xavier University in Chicago. The guys wanted to go downtown one night after an afternoon game, so I loaded up 12 kids and drove the 26 passenger Benedictine College Raven bus to the lakeside in downtown Chicago so that the kids could experience Christmas shopping on The Magnificent Mile. I couldn't find a parking space, so I dropped them off in front of Saks Fifth Avenue and told them I would meet them in 2 ½ hours in the same spot. My plan was to find a parking space and join them on the Mag Mile in an attempt to find something nice for my wife for Christmas. Unfortunately, Michigan Avenue has no place to park a 26-passenger bus, especially during the Christmas holidays. So, I ended up driving the bus up and down Michigan Avenue for 2 ½ hours until our prearranged pick-up time. I'm surprised that the police didn't pull me over to try to find out just what the hell I was doing driving up and down the Avenue. Fortunately, they didn't, and the kids had a good time shopping "in the city" while our school got some great "transit advertising" over Christmas in downtown Chicago!!

Beyond Being Coach Revisited

"Kindness is the language which the deaf can hear and the blind can see."
(Mark Twain, pen name for Samuel Langhorne Clemens, an American writer, humorist, entrepreneur, publisher, and lecturer.)

Following up on the father/grandfather theme, I believe all coaches go through situations where the players simply reach out for help because there is no one else to help them. I wouldn't say it was often, but a number of times each school year you had a kid who simply ran out of options and called you for help. Two instances come to mind:

One year I had a freshman athlete from St. Louis Vashon High School who used to go home practically every weekend to see his baby and his girlfriend. His name was Johnny Cooper. He was not only a really good athlete; he was also a really good person. "Coop" did not have a car, so he took the bus home each weekend during the off-season. Normally he would call one of two or three players who did have a car, and ask them to pick him up at the bus station upon his return to KC. (The bus did not travel to Atchison, which is about a 1-hour drive from downtown KC.) However, for one reason or another, there were a number of times when he could not reach anyone to come pick him up, so he would call me at 11 p.m. on a Sunday night and ask me if I could come get him. Now I'm a "10:30 to bed" type of guy, so the phone ringing at 11 p.m. was never a good sign for me. So I would get up, get dressed, and drive downtown to inner KC and get Johnny and take him to Atchison. It was a long night but leaving him at the bus station was simply not an option. It was really creepy being there at that time of night and was not safe for anyone to stay there overnight.

Unfortunately for our program, but fortunately for my beauty sleep, Johnny only lasted one year at BC. He was really good on defense – he was about 6'2" with long arms and extremely quick feet. Offensively he was not only quick, but fast. He played at a different speed than anyone else on the court. At times that wasn't so good – like the time at Baker University when we had the ball with about 5 seconds left and were down by 1 point. I had called time-out. Our Assistant Coach, Chic Downing, was at home listening to the game (he had a full-time job and couldn't travel with us very often) and told anyone there who would listen to him that we had better not let Johnny touch the ball – he'd throw it over the backboard! Well, although the play wasn't designed for Johnny to touch the ball, somehow he got it deflected to him and sure enough – his shot went over the backboard!!

I have lost track of Johnny these days – last I knew he was the starting quarterback for an Arena Football Team from St. Louis. But he is one "son" I will never forget (or dream about).

The other example of a kid in need involved a 30+ young man from California. One of my sons had played with him in an adult city league, and recommended I look at him. He was 6'2" but very thin. He was a very good outside shooter and played well on his visit to campus. Back in San Diego he worked at a Casino on their Security team. He did not make a lot of money, so he really did not have many funds to help pay for a private education. I gave him a modest scholarship, found a house directly across the street from campus to rent, and paired him with a juco transfer from Phoenix. Well, neither kid had any money, and the rental house was not furnished. So my wife, bless her heart, sent out a request at the community college where she worked in Kansas City asking for any furniture – beds, couches, chairs, chests of drawers, etc. that anyone could donate to help furnish their house. The response was excellent, and we were able to get most of the things they needed. So, I spent the next week or so driving around KC in my 1997 Ford Ranger pickup truck loading up furniture and driving it to Atchison. On one of the trips my wife and her mother, who happened to live in Atchison, accompanied me to the house. They noticed how frugal these kids were living, so they went out and bought a bunch of groceries and brought them back to the house for the kids.

Unfortunately, the juco player did not work out and left school at semester. That left the California kid alone in the house having to pay the full rent instead of just half the rent during the second semester. (As mentioned earlier, I tried to get the 7' kid to be allowed to move in with the California player, but the administration would not allow it.) This young man was a really good person – again, never complaining about his circumstances. He was not getting to play in games, since he did not make the top 13 or so players on the team, but he practiced hard every day. After the season ended, the owners of the house contacted me and said the rent had not been paid that month. When I talked to the player about it, he simply said he did not have any money left. I also found out that he was only eating one meal a day. I will admit something that only the player and my wife know – it's the only time I ever broke a NAIA rule, but I did when I wrote the kid a personal check so he could buy food and pay his rent. He was able to make it through the semester and return to California, where he got his job back at the casino. He did not return to BC, but today is actually coaching a men's team in southern California.

As I said earlier, these kids become your own emotionally and you do whatever you can to help them.

So, You Want to Be a Coach … Lesson #4:
Anticipate having to know more than just the fundamentals of your "Dream" field. Widen your vision and be prepared to address key issues that may not be an apparent part of your "Dream Job."

Chapter 5: The Fine Print

"Success means only doing what you do well, [and] letting someone else do the rest." (Goldstein's Truisms)

Like most jobs you inherit, there are miscellaneous responsibilities that are not necessarily spelled out when you assess the position. Here are some that I had not anticipated:

Bus Driver

"I think if you were to look at my resume in total you would see a lot of things that are kind of all over the map." (Don Cheadle, American Actor)

When I arrived at BC in the fall of 1998, most of the teams, except for football, used 15-passenger vans to travel to games. At the time I was 50 years old, and I don't remember ever driving a 15-passenger van. However, it was the responsibility of each sport's coach at BC to arrange for transportation. (Since budgets were minuscule, vans were the cheapest mode. The college did own a 26-passenger bus, but the football team used it until their season was over. After that the AD rotated who got to use the bus between volleyball, men's basketball, and women's basketball.)

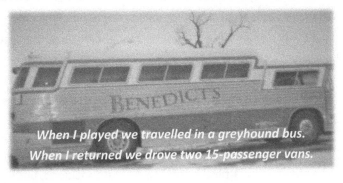

When I played we travelled in a greyhound bus. When I returned we drove two 15-passenger vans.

You have to know me to know how dangerous it is for me to be driving a team anywhere. It's not that I'm a bad driver - I'm actually a good driver. However, when I get on a highway, I become mesmerized by the road, and tend to find my head nodding, desperately wanting to have some nap time. When I sense the nodding coming on, I will turn up the radio loud and sing along. I'll roll down the windows and drive - even in the winter. I'll buy corn nuts, candy suckers, or anything else that will keep my mouth moving so I don't nod off.

With this flaw in my physical makeup, putting me behind the wheel of a van full of players was probably not a wise decision. So, when I got to BC, I made it known to folks that I would not be driving a van or bus to our away games. At first, I was successful and had been living up to that pledge. I was able to find a volunteer from town who had been a bus driver, had retired, and was willing to drive us to games. Also, the sportswriter for the local paper, the Atchison Globe, volunteered to drive a van to away games and thereby be able to cover our away games for the paper. So, my first year, I did not have to drive. Two things changed that during my second year - the retired bus driver died (naturally, not in an auto accident), and Jack, the sportswriter, frightened the players in his van so badly that they all tried to ride in the second van. We took 12 on the road plus a trainer and one or two of us coaches. (With all the equipment that accompanies the players, we required two vans for each trip)

> On one drive down to Springfield, Missouri, to play Evangel University in the playoffs, the van I was in was following Jack's van. We thought he was traveling too fast as he approached a turn in the road, and we were right. His van tried to negotiate the turn but went off the side of the road. Jack had that van on two wheels as he was rounding the curve, but somehow kept the van from overturning! When we got to Springfield, it was like watching the Keystone Cops as the players in Jack's van catapulted out of the side of the sliding doors. They were so happy to be on a solid surface that I thought a couple of them were going to kiss the ground! Well, that was the last time we asked Jack to drive the van for us.

I'd mentioned that the college did have a 26-passenger bus available for the basketball team's use after the football season concluded, but in order to drive it you needed to have a commercial driver's license (CDL). Well, that shouldn't be a big deal, but it was. Most coaches lived across the river in Missouri, so in order to get a CDL you had to have someone with a CDL drive you and the bus to St. Joseph, Missouri, to take the driver's test. If you ever watched the Seinfeld episode about "The Soup Nazi", you'll understand why I describe the guy at the St. Joe driver's test site as the "CDL Nazi." Stories of how he totally intimidated people, i.e., would be bus drivers, permeated throughout the coaching ranks. Passing the driver's test in a big bus was tough enough, but when you were done with that, you had to walk through a vehicle mechanical review with him, which was almost impossible to pass. He would name a part in the engine, and you'd have to point to that part and then describe its function. He'd ask what you would do if that vehicle broke down on the highway and XYZ was broken, and you were expected to know all the answers in order to pass the test. Now my dad or my brother would have had no problem with the CDL Nazi. They knew every part of every vehicle, what it did, and how to fix it. Not me - I had no interest in cars growing up. (How could you care about cars if there was some type - any type - of game going on in the neighborhood?) I decided since I was an imbecile when it came to auto mechanics, if the CDL Nazi were to ask me a mechanical question and wanted to know what I would do if the vehicle broke down, my answer would be "Call roadside assistance."

Fortunately for me, since I had recently moved from Missouri to Kansas, I could go to the CDL license testing facility in Kansas City, Kansas. YES!! I was able to dodge the St. Joe CDL Nazi. The KCK guy was a really nice person who was more interested in you driving safely than you being Joe Mechanic. He did ask a few mechanical questions, but they were simple ones that even I knew (like where is the radiator and how do you put water in it, where does the oil go, where do you put the windshield fluid?) So, I lucked out and was able to get a CDL after we lost our two volunteer drivers.

Was I a good bus driver? Kinda. I had one accident while driving the 26-passenger bus - I did not go wide enough on a right turn and scraped the side of the bus. It caused an ugly scratch and dent on the side, but no one was in danger of being hurt. Could someone have been hurt during my tenure of driving the bus? Yes. As I mentioned earlier, I have a tendency to be mesmerized by the road when driving and get very sleepy. The players used to take turns coming up to the front of the bus to talk to me, not because they wanted to engage in a meaningful conversation, but rather to keep me awake so they wouldn't perish in an auto accident on the way to or from a game. Some found it hard to sleep traveling on the way back from a game, for about every 45 seconds our tires would roll across the grooves in the road lining the side borders for highways here in the Midwest. I'm sure the players probably had wagers on how many times I would cause that noise to occur on a road trip. Between the players' front of the bus visits and my long cell phone conversations with our Arizona recruiting coach (two-hour time difference) who would talk to me all the way from St Louis to Atchison (five-and-a-half-hour drive), I was able to safely deliver our teams to and from games over the years. God really took care of all of us.

Weather conditions were another issue when it came to driving the bus. It seemed like every time we went to Graceland University (Bruce {Caitlyn} Jenner's alma mater in Lamoni, Iowa) there would be a blizzard on the way home. There also was the nightmare Ohio trip right after Christmas one year.

Some background - whenever I recruited an out-of-state player, I promised we'd play a game close to their home during their career so that their extended family and friends could come watch them play. Poochie Earl, my first recruit, was from Toledo, Ohio, so his junior year I scheduled Findlay University and Defiance University, both about 30 to 45 minutes from Toledo. I was blessed that year to have a good friend, Jerry Fennel, a lawyer from Nebraska who was a St. Benedict's grad one year before me, who took a year's sabbatical from his law practice and brought his wife down to Atchison where they worked for the college for a year. Jerry loved Raven basketball and asked if I'd like for him to drive the bus to some of our away games. After doing a backflip and saying, "you bet your sweet blank I would", Jerry got his CDL (not sure if he encountered the CDL Nazi or not) and became our bus driver that year. Since we were traveling to Ohio over Christmas break, Jerry was the designated driver. Well, we had one of those "once in 500-year" winter storms that hit just as we left Atchison. It took us 14 hours to get to St Louis, normally a five-and-a-half-hour drive. The storm followed us every inch of the way. The storm even stayed over St Louis overnight and accompanied us the remainder of the way to Ohio. (As a sidebar comment, one of my best friends, Bill Toepfer, said he watched the weather on TV and for two full days the radar had a small dot located right in the middle of the eye of the storm. He said it was our bus!!) We ended up having to postpone the Findlay game for a day, since we couldn't get there in time to play. On the way back, we were supposed to play Missouri - St Louis, and almost had to postpone that game also. The roads were pure ice on the way back. In Indiana, there was literally a 50-mile-long string of stopped traffic on I-70 heading east. Fortunately, we were heading west and the few cars that were going that way were mostly in the ditch. Jerry was able to keep that bus on that icy highway and get us to St. Louis safely. I have no idea how he survived that trip - he drove the whole way. But survive he did, and so did we, although after losing in OT to UMSL, we went 0-3 on the trip.

70

Weather conditions were also responsible for an incident that occurred after one of away games in KC. It really brought out the ingenuity of some of the kids I recruited from rural areas.

After playing a local college rival in KC, alumni Chuck and Marty Raplinger, whose son, Dan, had played for me for three years, invited us to their house for an after-game meal. They live in a lovely home in western KC that has a long winding driveway leading up to their house. We were in two 15 passenger vans at the time, so I drove one and an assistant drove the other. For some reason during the dinner one of the vans had to be moved. One of our Arizona players decided to grab the keys and move the van. Not knowing what it is like in Kansas after a heavy snow and then a thaw, he pulled the van off the paved driveway onto part of the yard. After all the festivities were over, all the players thanked the Raplingers and got into the vans. The van I was driving was parked on the driveway, so I had to turn it around in order to get back to the street. As I am driving down the driveway I look to my right to see the other van's tires mired about 6 inches into the wet ground. It was a mess. So all the kids from both vans got out and tried to push the stuck van back onto the driveway. It took about 15 minutes, but they were not successful. So I had to call a service who was able to pull the van out of the deep ruts it was mired in. We were all happy that we could finally get back on the road, but the downside was that our rental van had a huge dent in the back from where the guys were pushing.

I was blessed to have recruited a kid who could do practically anything. He grew up in rural Kansas, and anytime I struggled with something that had to be fixed or put together, Justin Long would volunteer to help me. He'd then very simply complete the project, while I would appreciatively look on. Well, that night Justin came to the rescue again. He asked me if I had a toilet plunger at my house. (Our house was located about 10 minutes from the Raplingers.) I said I did, so he asked if we couldn't stop by my house and he would guarantee that he could get the dent out for me. Now realize that it was about 12:30am, and my wife had long ago left the Raplingers to go home to go to bed. She was awakened by the phone call from her husband coach asking her if she would get the plunger and meet us at the front door. After realizing that this was not a dream/nightmare, she got the plunger and was waiting when I drove up. I got out, gave the plunger to Justin, who then thrust it against the back of the van and immediately pulled out the dent. It was amazing! He handed the plunger back to me and I to my wife, and the two vans were off again for the hour drive back to Atchison.

I learned a couple of lessons from this encounter: 1.) Never let an Arizona person get behind the wheel in the winter in Kansas, and 2.) Always recruit at least one kid from rural Kansas every four years.

Game Day Responsibilities - Home Games
"Other seed fell among thorns that grew up with it and choked out the tender plants." (Luke 8:7)

Game Days at home were always stressful, but not for the reason you might think. Yes, sure there were the butterflies you feel in your stomach before any game, home or away. But the stress from playing at home was due more to all that needed to be done to prepare the gym for the game than preparing for the opponent. Fortunately, two terrific faculty members, Lee and Angie Gomez, were as dependable as night following day – they took tickets at the gate and had been doing this for every football and basketball game for over 30 years. The head coach was responsible for practically everything else - pulling out the bleachers; placing the teams' chairs along the sidelines; setting up the control boxes for the scoreboard and the 35-second shot clocks; filling out the rosters and placing the official scorebook on the scorer's table (and don't forget the sharpened pencils); arranging for personnel to keep the scorebook and operate the scoreboard and the 35-second shot clocks; arranging for someone to sing or play a recording of the national anthem; arranging to get the checks printed and delivered to the referees (without looking like you were paying them off); ensuring the opponent's locker room was clean and a whiteboard and markers were moved into the locker room for their use; and arranging for a pre-game meal with the food services manager. It was amazing the number of times I had to find a singer or a 35-second shot clock operator 5 minutes before game time. Those two positions where the hardest to fill and not just anyone could step in and do those jobs.

Nellie in background with wife Amy looking amused.

I was blessed to have two wonderful volunteers, Nellie Regan and Bonnie Wagner (whose husband Danny was Mr. Raven – he was either a volunteer or a cheering participant in practically every athletic event on campus), to always run the scoreboard and keep the official book, respectively. Although Nellie, who I dearly love, never showed up until about 5 minutes before game time! He was always there to do the job, but never until the game was about to start. And

every game I'd be watching the door to see if Nellie was walking in, desperately hoping that this would not be the one night he did not make it on time. Nellie would do anything for me, but I do believe I turned a little gray up top a little before my time from watching that door.

The late, great Bonnie Wagner.

With all these responsibilities, it was practically impossible to concentrate on game preparation for the team on home-Game Day. However, there was one year when a new AD, Richard Konzem, took over all of these responsibilities and simply said "Coach, go coach. I'll take care of all game day preparations." Interestingly, we won 20 games that year, the only year we won 20 while I was there as a coach. Unfortunately, Richard left before the next year season, and all those responsibilities fell back on the head coach.

Raising Funds for Needed Improvements

"Money isn't the most important thing in life, but it's reasonably close to oxygen on the "gotta have it" scale." (Zig Ziglar, American Motivational Speaker)

Another requirement for me at BC was to raise money to supplement our operations budget and to fund any trips that I may want the team to take for holiday tournaments and the like. As I had mentioned, when I recruited an out-of-state player, which was quite often, I promised them and their parents that we would play a game close to their home at least once in the player's four years at Benedictine. When I started at BC in 1998-99, I recall my basketball budget being about $12,000 per year. This was not only to cover practice and game uniforms, travel expenses, recruiting, meals over Christmas vacation, etc., but also for game officials' fees (referees), telephone expenses, and any other expense incurred by the team or staff. Obviously, you can't run a college basketball program on $12K, so it fell upon the coach to raise the remainder required to field a team. In addition, the college did not want you to contact current college donors – they did not want you "stealing" their donors because your purpose was more "eye-catching" than their request for building improvements or endowment. So, we coaches were left to try to mine for donors who had not given to the college but supported us or our programs through some unique relationship. I really felt bad for my predecessor – he was not a BC grad and had few alumni connections, which was reflected in the state of the program's assets.

Uniforms

When I arrived, all college basketball teams' uniforms had trunks that the legs fell

1998-99 Team: Notice how low their waistline is?

at least to the knee, if not a tad below it. That was the style in 1998. BC's uniforms still had short pants, which the kids would pull halfway down their behinds so that the legs of the shorts would approach their knees. While

74

accomplishing the goal of getting the pants to approach the knee in length, unknowingly the players were actually combining two fashion looks – knee length shorts and what I will call (politically incorrect, I'm sure) the inner city look, where the folks wear their pants just below their butts and then their pant legs are all scrunched up on top of their shoes. You've seen that look, I'm sure. (I never really have understood that fashion statement. I tried it at home once to see what it was like. Having a belt at the base of my butt was extremely uncomfortable – plus my tighty whiteys were not near as attractive as the printed boxer shorts that are displayed for all to see when the waist of your pants are at the level they reach when you are about to, shall I say, relieve your body of the waste material that was not beneficial to fueling your body.) Anyway, before I allowed our kids to set a new fashion trend in basketball uniforms, I was able to raise enough money to buy new uniforms. We did not get them until the second year of my tenure, but at least it was only one year that I had to continually tell my players to "pull your pants up"!

If you thought the game uniforms were bad, you should have seen the practice uniforms. They may have been left over from the days when I played there. Again, it took the next season before we could replace these gems. To add insult to injury, each player had to buy their own shoes. We looked like the rainbow coalition when we took the floor. Through the generosity of many of my friends and alums, fortunately we were able to buy the players' shoes from then on, so that each player had a matching shoe. These were little improvements in the big picture of revitalizing a once proud program, but they were important. Players do not want to look weird. Most appreciate having cool looking uniforms – even practice uniforms. And I know for certain that they and their parents appreciated the basketball program buying their shoes for them. It not only raised the pride level of the current players; it eliminated a negative item from the recruiting agenda.

Holiday Trips

Our schedule was another area where additional fund raising was needed. The men's basketball program had not been on a holiday trip in many, many years.

Again, through the generosity of alums and friends we were able to schedule a trip to Florida my second year at the school. We played in a classic at Palm Beach Atlantic University in West Palm Beach, Florida, on a December

75

weekend, and then crossed the state and played Tampa University a few days later. It was such a treat for the kids. Some had never flown before, most had never been to Florida, and the experience of being on the road for 5 days or so in 80-degree weather instead of being on an empty campus in 20-degree weather was like heaven for them. Although we went 1-2 in Florida, the team bonded, which set the stage for a good second half of the season for us.

Speaking of the Florida trip, we did not get any funds for playing in Palm Beach's classic (so many teams want to come to Florida to play over the holidays that they do not need to pay anyone to play), but we did get $1000 from Tampa U. to offset some of our expenses. Tampa had a very good record that year and went to the NCAA Div. 2 Regionals, but, surprisingly, we gave them a pretty good game. They were one of 6 NCAA schools we played that year, all on the road. Four of the six made the NCAA Regionals. We went 0-6, which was expected, but were in every game except one. You are probably wondering why on earth would I schedule 6 bigger schools on their home courts. Wasn't I pretty well guaranteeing a 0-6 record? Yes, I was. But I was not concerned about our non-conference record. (We went 13-19 that year. Had I scheduled smaller schools, we could have possibly gone 6-0 and ended up 19-13.) You see, I believed that by playing teams that were more talented and had more scholarships than we had, it would mentally and physically prepare us to compete with the top teams in our league. Theoretically, we would not see anyone in our league as good as the best players from these NCAA schools. Plus, each school paid us to come play them, so I was able to subsidize our budget, but would have to sacrifice our record to do so. (In my last couple of years at BC, the rules changed, and you could count as many as three of your games as exhibitions, and therefore the result did not affect your overall record. Just so that you know, I never changed my belief in loading up good teams on our non-conference schedule. My last year at BC we played 6 NCAA schools. Three were exhibitions, and three were counted as regular season games. We lost the exhibitions but went 2-1 in the regular season games. The game we lost was by one point. In my mind, it was a testament to how far our program had come over the years.)

The "PIT"
In the years that followed, the NCAA road games helped add between $5K and $8K to our budget. Couple this with the generosity of our loyal donors, and we

were able to have a budget that was adequate for us to have a respectable program. The additional funds not only paid for the necessities, it also paid for facility improvements. One in particular was a tradition that had been part of Raven basketball for as long as anyone could remember, but was absent when I returned to BC in 1998-99. Every opponent that I ran into after graduating from college would curse our home court, especially "The Pit." You see, we played in an old gym that was state of the art in 1930. It was a second-floor gym, with spiral staircases leading down to the ground floor locker rooms. The gym had bleachers on the east side and permanent seats on the west side. On the south end was just enough room for two rows of classic wooden connected folding chairs, which were filled by the monks from St. Benedict's Abbey. Above the monks on the third story were "balcony" bleachers, where often the prison from Leavenworth or Lansing would bring prisoners to watch our games. They would sit on the east side of the balcony, and a band would sit on the west side of the balcony bleachers. Down at the north end of the gym, however, was "The Pit." It consisted of bleachers that stretched from sideline to sideline and rose up about 20-25 rows. That is where the craziest of the crazies stood – they very seldom sat – for the duration of every game. The tradition began many years earlier when the football team occupied these bleachers. When I played, the football program had been dropped, so the bleachers were filled with mostly "intoxicated" male students. (St. Benedict's was an all-guys school. Its sister school, Mt. St. Scholastica College, was an all-gals school across town. As a side note, if you were wondering, Benedict and Scholastica, in real life, were twins.) At the time, Kansas was an 18 state – which meant that you could buy 3.2% alcohol content beer when you were 18 years old. The Pit started yelling before warm-ups and never stopped. They totally intimidated the opponents, and it was not beyond them to say or do anything to further the Raven cause.

I remember one year we were playing one of our big rivals, Washburn University, and one of their students had the gall to run through the paper "hoop" before our team made its entry through that hoop into the gym. The Pit was furious, but we did not see any retaliation that was apparent. About the time of the first time-out, we looked over and saw every kid in the Pit waving a tiny piece of blue cloth. It took us a few minutes to figure it out, but that blue cloth had been a huge blue Washburn banner that had been hanging behind the opponent's bleachers. One of the Pit members snuck under the bleachers, pulled it down behind their fans, and snuck it over to the Pit. They then proceeded to tear it into the smallest of pieces so that each student in the Pit had a piece to wave at the Washburn team and crowd.

If you were a "Mountie" (that what we called the female students who attended Mount St. Scholastica), you would not dare walk in front of the Pit. Even though the gals sat in the section of the bleachers that were adjacent to the Pit on the east side of the gym, if they wanted to go to the west side, they always took the long way around. (So that you know, Mountie's were required to wear a skirt any time they left their campus, so all the gals had skirts on at our games.) If one was foolish enough to walk in front of the Pit, they were literally grabbed and passed up to the top of the Pit bleachers. The Pit had no shame.

Opposing players also were aware of the Pit's antics. They knew that if for some reason they happened to fly into the Pit chasing a ball or finishing a fast break layup, they weren't coming out without a few bruises, a few pinch marks, or even a bite or two. There was even a chance they may be passed up the bleachers like the Mounties. Except for one time.

> I was told this story by an AAU teammate of mine who played at Washburn shortly after I graduated from Benedict's. He was a little crazy himself and was known to play somewhat fearlessly. He said that one time he flew into the Pit trying to make a play, and to his astonishment, no one bit him, pinched him, or even punched him. He said they all were congratulating him on a great effort, patting him on the back, and helping him to remove himself from the Pit. He was utterly amazed and wondered if they had gone soft. His coach had called a time out on the play, so after escaping from the Pit unharmed, he trotted over to the team huddle and joined his coach and teammates. At first, they crowded around in the circle like normal, but soon moved away from him when they discovered the back of his jersey was covered with peanut butter. I'm telling you, those guys in the PIT were CRAZY!

To get back to the timeframe of when I had returned to BC to coach and found the new gym had no Pit, I questioned the folks and found out that when they built the new gym, they purposely left out bleachers at both ends of the court. There would be no more monks in folding chairs at one end, and crazy people at the other end. (Described by another AAU teammate of mine who had been a college opponent as "Heaven at one end, and Hell at the other"!) The AD who was in charge of the new building apparently had had enough trying to supervise the Pit during games and had tired of trying to explain the behavior of the Pit to the conference commissioner, I was told. So, he decided not to incorporate the Pit into the new gym's seating arrangement. From my perspective, it was a shame not to have such a great tradition continue. It was even awkward from a basketball court perspective, in that the south end of the court had about 30 feet of open space before you got to the wall of the gym. It was like something was missing – and that something was the PIT!

After a few years of coaching and raising funds for more needed purposes, we were able to raise enough money from our friends and alums to actually purchase bleachers for the south end of the court. It cost $30K, but I thought it was worth it. We weren't coming close to filling the bleachers on the sides of the court, but

that gaping hole at the end of the court just didn't look right. So, I was able to buy bleachers that spanned the width of the court, and right in the center

The New PIT.

of these bleachers were three huge red letters built into the black bleachers – you guessed it: P-I-T. It was a terrific addition ascetically, and I was hoping we could revive the spirit of the Pit and make home games an event again. Unfortunately, the new gym was now five years old and there was no student left on campus that had experienced the excitement of sitting (standing) in the Pit. You could tell all the war stories you wanted, and everyone on campus who was not a student had one, but that spirit was never revived.

It came close one year when one of the star football players, a huge 275 lb. 5' 9" lineman, became the Pit leader and got his football buddies to come out for our home games and get crazy. He would have fit in well in our day. He would come to the game in a kilt, and whenever an opponent would shoot a free throw, he'd do a handstand, exposing his decorative underwear! It was a riot – and the kids in the Pit had a great time at our games. And it made a difference to the team and to the student body. We actually had a home court advantage again, and more students started coming to games. Unfortunately, the Pit leader was a senior, and after he graduated, no one stepped up to take his place.

The Pit to this day is still there, but the spirit has not returned – at least not at the games I have attended. A few students sit in this section, but there is no harassing of opponents, no antics to distract the focus of the opposing team, and very little cheering. Maybe it's a sign of our times. Kids today seem to be more focused on a small screen that fits in their hand than they are in what is happening in the real world. It seems to me that it is less important to have a good time with your friends and more important to send your friends a photo of you acting like you are having a good time.

Locker Room

The last big item that our donors were able to provide to the program was a first-class locker room. I really wished I could have been around when the new gym was built. There were a number of items that I would have strongly recommended, and one of them was a good locker room for the home teams (men and women). Whoever designed the gym made all four locker rooms exactly the same. All had about 30 or so steel lockers. All had the same number of toilets and showers. All were the same size. Now logically speaking, how often do your visiting locker rooms get used compared to your home locker rooms? Wouldn't it make sense to make the home locker rooms bigger and customize them to cater

to the home teams? And how many teams, even home teams, have 30 plus players? My challenge was to create an attractive and functional locker room out of one in which the walls could not be moved – they were all concrete  walls. The first thing that had to be accomplished was to get the administration to agree that the basketball team did not need to have 22 – 24 players. Fifteen players would have been plenty. (Since the college was doing an excellent job of recruiting regular students, there no longer was a need for the basketball team to recruit all the additional players just to help with enrollment numbers.)

I was able, in my last two years, to get agreement from the administration that we could cut down the squad size. With that done, I could now proceed with the refurbishment project. I hired a local cabinet maker to come in and design 18 beautiful stadium lockers. He used a birch wood with cherry wood stain. The stadium lockers gave each player his own large locker where he could hang up his practice or game uniforms, store any valuables in either the wide seat that stored his shoes, etc. or a small locker with a combination on it that was above the area where he hung his clothes. It had to be the nicest locker of any small college basketball locker rooms. A great friend of the college and great friend of mine, Pat Regan (aka Nellie, our game timekeeper), had his own carpet business. He tore out our old carpet and put in some great indoor/outdoor carpet that helped highlight the new lockers. We bought a 60-inch TV and mounted it above a custom cabinet at one end of the locker room, and within the guts of the cabinet were storage areas and a place for our two large plastic garbage barrels that held the previous practice's soiled uniforms and towels (effectively keeping these eye sores out of sight and smell). When the kids returned from summer break, they were in awe of their new locker room. It was first class, and they knew and appreciated it. It turned out to be a good recruiting tool also, because no other team in our league had anything that compared to it. Oh, and by the way, we named the locker room after our beloved basketball Chaplain, Fr. Hugh Keefer. (Interestingly, neither the AD nor the President ever

Richard Konzem and wife Deb help celebrate my 60ᵗʰ Bday

commented to me concerning the locker room improvements, but the Prez did compliment Fr. Hugh on having a "urinal" named after him!☺)

Coaches Offices
In the midst of the gym improvements we also had a significant improvement in

81

coaches' offices. Our new AD, Richard Konzem, was a man with great vision. He came to us after rising to the highest assistant AD position at the University of Kansas. When KU hired a new AD (Richard was a strong candidate but did not get the job), he found himself on the outside. KU moved him to be the director of the Dole Center, which was a prestigious position that was responsible for bringing in high profile speakers to the Lawrence campus. Richard did a good job at the Dole Center, but his heart was in athletics. After a couple of years of being out of athletics, to the benefit of Benedictine College, BC hired Richard as their Athletic Director. He was far and away not only the most qualified AD we had ever had, in my opinion, he was also the most effective. He really knew how to manage groups of people, especially coaches.

Richard had the idea to move the workout area above the coaches' offices in the new gym, which housed the nautilus equipment, into a space he would create on the ground floor of the old gym. He then would create an office suite for the basketball coaches and the AD in the space that was cleared by removing the nautilus equipment. He had planned to send out a letter to all basketball alums and seek the $50,000 it would take to make these moves and furnish the new offices. He was working with the Director of Advancement at BC to make this happen when he came to me and asked if I knew of anyone who could finance this project themselves. I told him that the only one I knew of that would have a strong connection to basketball and the wherewithal to fund the project was a friend and teammate of mine from our 1967 National Championship team, Jack Dugan. Jack had had a very successful career as an ophthalmologist in Texas. His father, John T. Dugan, was the one who actually recruited me to St. Benedict's back in 1966, and Jack was one of the reasons I chose to attend SBC. I told Richard and the

Director of Advancement that if we named the basketball suite after Jack's dad, who had recently died, that he may just go ahead and do the whole project. Well, the Director of Advancement called Jack and floated the idea of Jack funding the suite. Jack said he'd like to

Jack Dugan at new suites dedication

do it, but he had already committed a large donation that year to another charitable organization. He thought maybe he could do it in the next year or two when that commitment ended. The director told Jack that she understood his position, but then added that we were planning on calling it the "John T. Dugan Basketball Suite." When Jack heard this, he had second thoughts and asked the Director if he could have a few days to think it over. A couple days later he called and confirmed that he would do the project that year. We were obviously excited about the prospect of having new offices (with new furniture) that overlooked the gym floor. It was a perfect place for the basketball offices. So, during the summer prior to the start of the new school year, the new space was created for a workout area for the student body in the old gym, the equipment was moved, new equipment was added, and the basketball suites were constructed and furnished in the new gym. The new suite gave a very professional appearance and added to the quality of both basketball programs. Unfortunately for us, Richard accepted another AD position at an NCAA school prior to actually moving into the office in the suite that he created for the AD. Losing Richard was a real blow to the athletic program, for he had not only helped the basketball programs improve, he had done the same thing for all the other programs at the school.

BC decided to promote the assistant AD, an assistant football coach, to become the new AD. Since the football coach already had an office at the football complex, and he would continue coaching football as well as being the AD, it freed up the AD's office Richard had built in the new gym for the women's volleyball coach. She moved up to the new office from her office on the gym floor, so she and her program ended up benefitting from the generosity of the Dugan family.

For us, the new offices gave our programs real legitimacy when recruits and their parents came to visit. We had a beautiful place to bring them to and have a nice sit-down visit with them and could do it in a setting that overlooked the court we hoped they would be playing on in the future. Now we had great offices for the coaches and a great locker room for the players. Facilities would no longer be a detriment to our recruiting efforts.

So, You Want to Be a Coach ... Lesson #5:
Know that wearing the "Dream Hat" may require you to make it fit sideways, backwards, and upside down.

Chapter 6: Challenges

Recruiting

"The thing that drives most coaches out of coaching in college is they get tired of the grind of recruiting." (Bobby Bowden, College Hall of Fame football coach)

I both loved and hated recruiting. I loved when potential student-athletes would come to campus for an official visit. It was an opportunity to showcase our facilities, but more importantly, our hospitality. The Benedictine religious order which founded the college is known for its hospitality, and that virtue permeated itself throughout the entire College. From students to faculty to staff, everyone made visitors feel welcomed and wanted. Our experience was that if we could get a recruit to visit our campus, we stood a good chance of signing him.

The Good Stuff

"All altruism springs from putting yourself in the other person's place." (Harry Emerson Fosdick, American pastor)

I especially enjoyed on campus recruiting visits when one or both parents accompanied the recruit. Having raised two sons myself who played college basketball and earned college degrees, I found it very easy and comfortable to talk about the decision facing the family concerning the next four years of their precious child's life. Most parents are interested in much more than just basketball when it comes to making a college choice. The level of Education, the types of jobs

The Hunds, Johnsons & Corlesses: great parents and great supporters.

graduates get, and how financing works were some of the major concerns of parents that the recruits themselves did not always consider. Having the time to discuss these in detail with a parent was invaluable. It also gave me a chance to talk about spirituality on campus and in our program. Even though BC was a very traditional catholic College, most of my players were not Catholic. (With no recruiting budget, limited-time opportunities to travel on recruiting trips, limited basketball scholarships, and no direct connection between Catholic colleges and Catholic high schools, being "choosy" and making a recruit's religious affiliation a high priority was not an option.) Most parents supported the idea that their son would be exposed to a community that valued spiritual life and one's soul. Making sure that they understood that we did not put pressure on non-Catholic students to become Catholic also resonated well with both recruits and their parents. I did, however, let the recruit and the parents know that I personally made God a part of our basketball program by engaging the team in prayer before every practice and before and after every game. I also talked about doing the "right thing" both on and off the court. I wanted to make sure that these young men understood that it was okay to be male and spiritual. It was okay to be a man and to pray. It was okay to be a man and have a Faith Life. It was okay to be a man and be a spiritual leader. (Hopefully the seed that was planted back then will sprout and flourish as these young men become fathers and grandfathers themselves.)

Not All parents Are Alike

The parents who did not relate well to this type of recruiting visit were the ones who were living vicariously through their sons. And in almost all cases, these were fathers who felt that they personally fell short of their athletic dreams as a young person. You see these dads at every level. They are ones who volunteer to coach your children. They are ones who show favor to their own child over more qualified teammates. They are ones who push their kid relentlessly, when many times all the kid wants to do is to have fun playing ball with his friends. They are ones who try to win at all costs, rather than spending time teaching the youngsters the fundamentals that will form the foundation of future success.

> At our level I didn't run into these types of dads often but there were some. I recall a father of one of our freshman players whose 6'9" brother was playing NCAA division 1 basketball. There was a coaching change at the D1 school, and the brother was let go by the new coach. The family was in the process of visiting NCAA division 2 schools that were candidates for their D1 transfer son. Since little brother (6'4") was already at BC and getting some playing time as a freshman, they agreed to visit. The visit was going fine until we started talking about postgraduate opportunities. I made a statement that our graduates got good jobs after earning their degree, and that in the history

of our school we had yet to have a science degree major (biology, chemistry, etc.) not get accepted into medical or dental school. (This was a remarkable record, and a real testament to the excellent job done by our science faculty.) The dad, who wasn't thrilled about his son going from NCAA D1 to NAIA D2, scoffed at my remark and simply said he didn't believe me. I graciously assured him that what I said was true, but the remainder of the visit was somewhat strained. Since the dad really wanted the brothers to play together in college, we now stood a good chance of not only losing the transfer recruit to another school, but also losing his less talented brother from our program.

As it turned out, the division 1 transfer signed at a NCAA D2 school, which was okay. What wasn't okay was that the dad insisted that the younger brother transfer to the same school. Now I knew the NCAA D2 school was not interested in the least in our freshman player, but they would let him "walk on" if they could sign the 6'9" brother. I also knew that the younger brother would never see the court at the NCAA D2 school, for that school had just joined one of the top NCAA D2 leagues in the country. Younger brother simply was not good enough to play consistently in that league. I tried to counsel the younger brother on these facts, but his father's influence was too strong, so he transferred anyway. And, you guessed it, he never got to play for the NCAA D2 School. As a sidelight, I refused to release the younger brother from his commitment to BC, so he had to redshirt one year at the new school. This infuriated the dad, but I thought that this would be a good life lesson for the player, i.e., decisions have consequences. My experience with 18 to 22-year olds was that they did not always hold themselves accountable for their decisions. I constantly "preached" to do the right thing. In your heart you know what the right thing is. Doing the right thing and then living with the consequences of our decisions is justifiable, and bearable, if the consequences turn out to be negative. For me it was the same way in business. I personally tried to follow this belief and espoused it among the people who I worked for, with, and especially who worked for me.

As for the decision to release the younger brother from his commitment to BC, that was a policy of the school. It could be overridden by the AD, but I strongly recommended not to override it in this case. I had two reasons: the first, as mentioned above, was to use this as a life lesson for the player, and the second was that the young man, even if he dreamed of playing at the D2 school, would need to redshirt a year to learn their system and to figure out what he needed to do physically to be good enough to play there. By not releasing him from his BC commitment I guaranteed that he would have to be red-shirted and would have a year to grow into their program.

The Not-So-Good Stuff
"He that can't endure the bad will not live to see the good." (Yiddish proverb)

I've talked about some of the things I loved about recruiting, now let me mention some of the things I hated about it.

Time
Finding time was my number one dislike. Summertime was not a problem, since my only academic commitment was teaching an Executive MBA class on Friday nights. Finding the time during the season, though, was a major problem. In our area, high schools played games on Tuesday and Friday nights. Our college games were on Thursdays and Saturdays, with an occasional Monday game thrown in. Preparing a team for two or three games a week was challenging - many hours are spent reviewing film and preparing a game plan. With class schedules being what they were, team practice was about the only time you had to communicate the game plan to the team. Therefore being at practices was mandatory for me. Sending an assistant was not an option either my first 10 or 11 years, since in the earlier year's my assistant coach had a full-time job outside of the college and in my later years my assistant was a graduate student who had classes at night. Once the grad assistant graduated and was able to travel, he did not have a reliable vehicle to use. The college did not have cars that could be used for this purpose, so it was risky sending a young assistant on the road in the wintertime in Kansas with an unreliable vehicle. In addition, we had no budget to pay for the recruiting trip expenses. On top of all of that, even if one of us two coaches could go recruit, the other would be left to run a practice with 22 to 24 players. Getting the varsity ready for their next game while not having 12 to 14 guys standing around watching was quite a challenge.

I'm "D1"
Another thing that bugged me about recruiting was the attitude of the local high school players. Since BC had not been successful in basketball since shortly after my playing days there, their basketball reputation was very poor. The local Kansas

City High School players either had not heard of the school, or they were not interested in a losing program.

The recruiting protocol at a high school game was to wait until after the game and stand outside the locker room until the high school player emerged. Normally there were three to six coaches (most of them assistant coaches from jucos or small schools) waiting to talk to the player. You basically got in line and waited your turn. More often than not, when I approached a player and introduced myself and my school to them, as soon as they found out we were an NAIA D2 school, their eyes began to wander. Many simply weren't interested in BC or NAIA D2, and even though they had never seen our team play, their attitude was that if you started on a Kansas City High School team, you'd be a star at the NAIA D2 level. Even though that attitude frustrated me, you could not let that frustration show when you were talking to the player. You simply had to be gracious, make your pitch, and hope that the kid "liked" you enough to reply to any follow-up efforts. (It slayed me that most kids thought they were D1 material. The jucos thrived on this, telling them that if they came to a Juco for one or two years, they'd sign at a D1 school. What really happened was that these kids ended up simply filling out the juco roster with the mandatory number of home state players, while watching the out-of-state players get all of the playing time. The sad thing is that after sitting on the bench for 2 years of Juco, the same kid you were interested in out of high school would contact you looking for a 4-year school to transfer to after their juco eligibility ended. In almost every case, I had to tell them I was not interested any longer. They not only hadn't played much in two years, they also had most likely picked up some bad basketball habits and had taken many courses that would not transfer to BC. Getting them eligible was difficult and paying for 3 years of school for 2 years of eligibility was not a good option.)

Scholarships
An additional thing I hated about recruiting was our scholarship restrictions. We had six full scholarships spread over 22 - 24 players. That meant everyone had to pay something to play at BC. Even if you gave a player full tuition scholarship (say $20,000), they still had to come up with room, board and books (say $10,000). How do you convince a good player to sign with you if he can be an invited walk-on at a more prestigious state school and actually pay less to walk on than if he

accepted your scholarship? I can't tell you how many local players we lost to that scenario.

You can probably guess that our roster did not contain many local players. We had to rely on out-of-state student athletes to fill out our Varsity roster. I'm sure you are thinking "Wouldn't you have the same problem scholarship-wise with out-of-state recruits?" Actually, no. We recruited heavily in Arizona. At the time Arizona only had four 4-year schools. All of the rest of the schools were junior colleges. Three of the four 4-year schools were NCAA D1 and the other (Grand Canyon University) at the time was an NCAA D2 school. That meant that any good Arizona players not recruited by the four 4-year schools had to go out of state or go to a 2-year school and then transfer out-of-state after two years. That gave us an in.

Fortunately, I had a very good friend (Van Van Dyke) who had migrated from Collinsville, Illinois to Phoenix, and he loved and knew basketball. I hired him for $0 (a very good friend, indeed!) as an assistant coach, and he became our

head Arizona recruiter. He would watch approximately a hundred high school games a year, and because of his efforts, we were able to graduate 13 Arizona kids from our program during my tenure. They all were among our most talented players. Without that pipeline, we would not have won even 20% of our games, in my opinion. Because there were

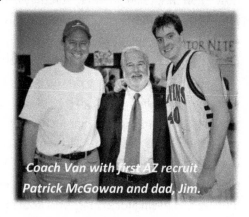

Coach Van with first AZ recruit Patrick McGowan and dad, Jim.

so many Arizona kids going out of state to school, paying part of their educational expense became a reality to the parents. This fact allowed us to be competitive with other out-of-state schools. (The only caveat was that our school had a rule that you could only pay $75 towards public transportation for a recruit to visit. This eliminated some of our targeted recruits, since flying from Phoenix or Tucson to Kansas City was normally around $300, of which the recruit would have to pay about $225. My last 2 years at the school I was able to convince the president and AD that this policy really hurt our recruiting, for as I said before, if we could get a student-athlete to visit campus, we stood a good chance of signing him. The president and AD allowed me during my last 2 years to pay the full fare, as long as I raised the money for it. With this change in policy we were able to recruit and sign the Arizona Juco Regional MVP, a 6-6 forward, my first year. The second year of the policy change we signed a NCAA D1 transfer, a 6'2" scoring guard. {Unfortunately, he opted out of his signed commitment with BC after they fired me. Instead, he played for another NAIA school and led the nation in scoring!} Without the policy change, neither player would have visited BC, much less signed with us.)

Bottom line - the change in scholarship limits (my last two years we moved to NAIA D1 and were stair-stepped to 9 scholarships over the next 3 years) and the change in public transportation reimbursement policy put us on a <u>Level Playing Field</u> with the top schools in our conference and most small school's nationally. These two policies allowed us to remove two huge shackles and made us a competitor on the recruiting trail.

Feedback

One other thing about recruiting that was interesting was finding out some of the reasons why some kids who visited signed with us while others did not.

There was a guard from St. Louis who was at an NCAA school but wanted to transfer. He had graduated from a Catholic High School before playing one year at the NCAA D2 school. We were aware of him in high school but were not one of his choices for college at the time. When we found out that he wanted to transfer, we were able to get him to come visit. The visit went well. He liked the campus, had a good time with our players Saturday night, and played well when he and our players played on Saturday afternoon. He ended up not signing with us, so I called his high school coach to try to gather information as to his former player's reason for not choosing us. The high school coach was, fortunately, very frank - he said the young man had an enjoyable visit, he liked the coaching staff and the players, and he liked the campus, too. However, he could not see himself at BC because of the "Roadkill"! Apparently, he noticed all the roadkill on Highway 45 when we were driving from KCI Airport to campus - about a 45-minute drive. (The kid was right - it's amazing how many opossums, raccoons, deer, etc., you see on this stretch of road, especially the 15-mile stretch that runs along the

Missouri River and an Eastern Ridge that parallels the river.) We had lost kids for a number of reasons before, but this was indeed the most unique and bizarre reason that I had come across.

Diversity By-Product

"Friends are relatives you make for yourself." (Eustache Deschamps, French poet)

One of the positive things about recruiting out-of-state players was the opportunity to meet young men from all over the country. We had players from New York, California, Florida and the state of Washington. Our varsity roster

2009-10 players from MO, KS, OH, CO, NY & AZ

consisted of players from all around the country. Each brought a unique perspective, or culture, if you'd like, to the team. The NY kids were normally much less laid back than the California kids. We had blacks, whites, Hispanics, Islanders, Australians and even a Serbian and a Polish kid. One of the cool things to witness was the bonding that occurred among such a diverse group of young

men. The first showing of this normally happened at Thanksgiving. We usually played on the Saturday after Thanksgiving, so I would allow the team to go home after practice on Wednesday and the varsity reported back on Friday afternoon. It was heartening to see the local players invite the players from a distance to come home with them for Thanksgiving. I often thought about how rewarding it would have been (in most cases) for the parents of the local kids to host someone from a distant city. The conversations would not be the normal Thanksgiving conversations. The food and camaraderie, from the distance player's perspective, would have been great, I'm sure. (You remember cafeteria food, don't you?). What I observed many, many times was sort of an adoption by the local parents of the distance players. Now when the parents came to watch their son play, they actually had two or maybe even three kids to watch and cheer on. And if you think games were fun to observe, you should have been there on graduation day.

The best thing about the whole situation was the fact that a life-long bond had been created, so that now when you go to a wedding or a baptism or some other family type of event, who do you see there but the adopted parents. In a nutshell, that is what BC was all about – relationships.

The personalities of the recruits varied significantly, as you can imagine. I felt like a father to most of them, and toward the end of my tenure like a grandfather. And like any father, you learned to enjoy certain things about all of your kids.

One of my favorite players was a young man by the name of RJ Demps. He was a point guard from a Catholic high school in Denver. He led his team to the state championship his senior year. We ended up recruiting him based on a phone call from a good friend of mine, Jay Eveler, who lived in St. Louis and happened to be watching the Colorado state high school championships on TV. He called me about RJ, and said he knew one of the assistant coaches at the high school and told me I

RJ DEMPS

should contact the coach about this kid. I took his advice and found out that RJ had not earned the minimum score yet on the ACT entrance exam. He also was only 5' 9" tall, so there weren't a slew of colleges after him. After watching film of RJ, and seeing how intense he played the game, I invited him to campus for a visit. He came from Denver with his family and had a great visit. Although he was only 5'9" tall, he weighed about 190 lbs. and was simply a tough kid on the court. Off of the court, he had the most infectious smile – it was on his face all the time. You couldn't help but love RJ. We made an offer and he accepted, but since he hadn't qualified on the ACT exam, he had to redshirt his freshman year. That was my last year coaching at BC, unfortunately. I never got a chance to coach him in a game – but we sure had some interesting moments in practice. One in particular stands out – it was shortly before Christmas break and he was playing against the varsity in a full court drill. His team had the ball in transition, and he was cutting toward the ball at midcourt when his teammate fired a bullet of a pass to RJ. The pass caught RJ's pinky and simply made the finger stand straight up. RJ was a tough kid, but when he saw his little finger standing straight up, he freaked out. He started screaming "My finger! My finger!" and running around like a chicken with its head cut off (for you farm vets). I tried to calm RJ as I approached him, but he just kept screaming "My finger! Ohhh, my finger!" The next thing I knew, he jumped onto my chest and wrapped his legs around my waist and started biting my shoulder. Now I started screaming "My shoulder! My shoulder!" Envision, if you will, being one of our other players on the court watching your head coach and a teammate dancing around the court screaming "My finger! My finger – My shoulder! My shoulder!" Fortunately, the trainer came running onto the court and was able to pry RJ off my body and calm him some by popping the finger back to its original position. I must say that in all my experiences in the business world, none prepared me for that scenario.

[A sad side note – two years later, after I had been replaced, RJ was driving to the KC airport early one morning after returning to Atchison from a road game in St. Louis. He was trying to get to the airport very early in the morning so that he could get a standby ticket to return home for Christmas. On his way to KCI his car slid on black ice and careened off the road and down a steep embankment. RJ was killed in the crash. Going to his funeral and burial was one of the hardest and saddest moments of my life. I loved that kid.]

Good Advice Not Followed
"The man who claims he never made a mistake in his life generally is married to a wife who did." (Anonymous)

Another positive about recruiting was meeting and getting to know the parents of our players. This may sound odd to some, especially high school coaches, but at the college level parents are a positive thing in most cases. One reason is that they are not co-located in almost all circumstances (especially if your college is located in Atchison, Kansas!). Unlike high school, the parents do not normally know the coach or his family, the administration, the other parents, or those of influence at the college. They are cast into a position of trusting the coach and his staff, as well as the faculty and college staff, to not only develop their son as a basketball player, but especially as a young person growing into a man. This opportunity was one of my favorite things about coaching at the college level. You get a boy of 18 and do your best to turn him into a man of 22. Along the way, you will have interactions with the parents. Almost always these are positive encounters. Many are caused by something good happening (good game, good grade report, etc.), but some stem from negative circumstances (injury, bad grades, disciplinary situation). In all cases, I found that if you were sincere about helping their son "do the right thing" or "make an informed decision", the parents were nearly 100% supportive. These experiences created a relationship between the coach and the parent – and that relationship was never more apparent than on senior night (last home game of the season) and again on graduation day.

I was blessed to have some very understanding parents. In only one instance in my 12 years as a head coach did I have a parent who didn't get it, in my opinion. Interestingly, he was the dad of one of my most talented players during my 12-year tenure. This father had done a great job of developing his son's basketball skills. The kid could literally shoot as well left-handed as he could right-handed. (Shortly after he arrived, I had him shoot 25 shots from 3 locations behind the three-point line lefty, and three more spots righty. Out of 25 from each spot, he hit at least 21 both left-handed and right-handed. It was amazing.) Plus, he had the best "handles" of anyone I had coached. The ball was just part of his hand. His downside was his 5' 10" height, he was a step slow for NCAA D1, and he was selfish on the court. Being a point guard, he had a major influence on how the rest of his teammates played. Unfortunately, in my opinion he never learned that his job was to make them better, not to make himself look great. You are probably wondering how we could have signed such a talent, since we were limited on scholarships and had no recruiting budget. Well, my high paid recruiter in Arizona (my buddy Van) had heard of him and went to see him play. He recognized the talent level and started a dialogue with him and his father. Ironically, I was attending my son's bachelor party in Las Vegas at the same time this young man was playing in the post-high school season tournament held each year in Vegas. I was able to grab one of my son's great b-ball friends who was also attending the bachelor's party, and we went to watch the kid play. (Fortunately, it was the first day of the bachelor's party.) We both agreed that the kid had a lot of talent, but we disagreed on recruiting him. (My son's friend, Jeff McCaw, was a very good college and AAU point guard, and was now coaching high school in St. Louis. One of his sons, who was about 2 years old at the time, later became a member of the Golden State Warrior's 2017 & 2018 and Toronto's 2019 NBA championship teams, so Jeff knew his stuff.)

95

Jeff recommended that I not recruit him. His reasoning was simple: "look at the faces of his teammates," Jeff said. "None of them are enjoying playing with him. He is selfish and hurts the team more than his talent helps them." I agreed with Jeff's assessment, but said "Jeff, I can change that kid." Having been a point guard myself, I was sure I could teach the young man how to become unselfish, and to use his skills to make everyone better on the team. I was wrong. His most productive year, in my opinion, was his sophomore year, when I moved him to the two-guard position and started him with four strong-willed seniors. They controlled him, and he had a great year, as did they. However, the next year with the seniors gone, the young man returned to his old ways. Finally, during his senior year he was part of a 5-in 5-out 10-man rotation I used. He fit well with the 5-man group he played with. They pressed and pushed the ball on offense (whereas the other 5-man squad played a match-up zone and ran a disciplined patterned offense). On senior night, with his dad in the stands, I kept the "patterned" squad on the court from about the 10-minute mark of the second half until about two minutes remaining in the game. The game was one we had to win to stay in contention to qualify for the league playoffs, and the patterned group had built up a 15-point lead with 5 minutes to go in the game. I made the decision to leave them in because of how well they were playing and the fact that they limited the number of possessions because of their style of play. With two minutes left and a 13-point lead, I subbed in the other 5-man group. They quickly lost 7 of the 13-point lead, through rash carelessness, primarily by this young man. He was playing like he couldn't care less if we won or lost. With seconds left in the game, the other team was shooting a technical foul due to one of our players saying something to one of their players, and the opponent had a chance to actually beat us if they hit the free throws and made a 3-point shot on the inbounds play. Fortunately, they missed the 3-pointer and we won. However, I was not a happy camper, and let the seniors know it in the locker room. This was so unlike all the other senior nights we had. They were always happy affairs – this one wasn't.

After releasing the team from the locker room, I walked outside the locker room to see this young man leaving the gym. (Later I had a person tell me they overheard his dad telling him that he was "done.") All the other players stayed to have pictures taken, etc. My wife, who drove from KC to attend our home games, was leaving the gym when she saw this young man crying, sitting on a small hillside just outside the gym. When she asked him what was wrong, he said "Nothing." At that point his dad came up and harshly said "Get Up! We are going."

We had one day to practice before having to take a 5-hour bus ride to play our last game of the season against Culver Stockton University. Again, in order to qualify for the playoffs, we had to win this road game. A couple of hours before the Friday practice this young man came in to tell me that he was quitting the team. I was astounded. He had played nearly 4 full seasons, was a starter for most of his career, and with one game to go in his senior year he was going to quit? When I brought up the question of his dad's involvement in this decision, he told me his dad had nothing to do with it and I should leave his dad out of the conversation. He then proceeded to tell me how bad of a coach I was. He said, "You are a good man, but you are a horrible coach." The hairs on the back of my neck stood straight out, and I wanted to personally rip into him about his selfishness, etc., but I knew in my heart that that was not the right thing to do. So, I just smiled and listened. When he was done, I told him I would honor his request and asked him to clean out his locker. I never got confirmation that this young man was forced to quit by his dad, but I'm sure the father was a major influence on the decision. For me, it went against everything I had ever been taught about "toughing it out." You don't quit – you persevere. Regardless of how tasteless the situation (unless it involves something that is unsafe, immoral or illegal), you make the best of it until the time comes when you can move on graciously. From that standpoint, I had also failed in developing this young man.

Well, the next day I drove the bus on the 5-hour trip to Canton, Mo., contemplating how to adjust the team to playing a normal substitution system rather than the 5-in, 5-out rotation I had used for most of the season. I only had one true point guard, Dave Goettelmann, and he was a freshman. He had been playing with the "pattern" group most of the year and did a good job with them. He was a very heady player, and even though he was only 5'10" and 155 lbs. soaking wet, he was mentally tough. To make a long story shorter, he had a great game – 10 points, 8 assists, 1 turnover in about 35 minutes. And we won on the road. It was one of the most satisfying victories, for me, in my 12 years. I loved how everyone stepped up and did whatever it took to win. I was very proud of them.

As for the player who quit, he and I did not see each other much after the season ended. He did graduate, but I don't remember seeing him or his family at graduation. I did not see him until the funeral of Fr. Hugh, our chaplain, about 5 or 6 years after the player graduated. I was surprised to see him there, although I know he and Fr. Hugh had a good relationship. When I saw him, I decided it was time for me to make the first move and attempt a reconciliation. So, after the service, I went over to him and told him how much it would have meant to Fr. Hugh to know he was there, and that I appreciated his making the effort to attend the weekday funeral. He responded favorably and even called me "Coach"! The monastery had a luncheon after the service, and I was able to spend time with him and find out where his life had led him since school. It was great to hear that he had settled in the KC area and he had his own Insurance Agency. Since that time, he has married and has a successful business – so the story has a happy ending. As far as the dad is concerned, I don't know what his status is, but I am sure he is also proud of what his son has become.

To my recollection, that is the only negative experience I had with a parent while coaching. There may have been others that I have forgotten, but none significant enough for me to recall. Practically all my parental relationships' memories are of attending their sons' weddings, etc. They were good parents who raised good kids.

From a Business Perspective
"Unless you find some sort of loyalty, you cannot find unity and peace in your active living." (Josiah Royce, American Idealist philosopher and teacher)

In business we seldom have to deal with related parties, especially parents. Spouses may get involved periodically with situations at work, but normally that is not the case. If it is, then my approach would have been the same as my approach to the players' parents, i.e., I would make sure they knew that I was committed to do "the right thing" and to keep the employee's best interests at heart.

One thing I did do in business that involved family was to privately reward people who worked in my organization when they "took the extra step" and went beyond what their job description called for. I would buy a gift certificate to a nice restaurant and ask them to privately come to my office with their direct boss, where I would present the certificate to them and thank them for such loyalty to the firm and to their commitment to excellent service. I acknowledged that their sacrifices for the firm came at the expense of their family at times, and that I appreciated the family's support of the employee. I would then encourage them to take their family to dinner as a token of our appreciation. We never announced these rewards publicly – it was something personally between me and the employee, and for me, it was a way to show sincere appreciation for a job done well.

So, You Want to Be a Coach ... Lesson #6:
Working with people is a huge part of coaching. Invest early in honing your people skills.

Chapter 7: Similarities & Differences Between Business Management and Coaching

"We are all alike, on the inside." (Mark Twain, American writer)

When I was managing at Southwestern Bell, I often found myself equating work situations with athletic situations. I didn't have any scientific studies or proof of the close relationship managing had with coaching, but I truly felt that there was a close bond between the two. After experiencing both for extended periods of time I found that I was right, and simultaneously I was also wrong. Some scenarios lend themselves well to both work and athletic situations, and some scenarios do not. Let me explain what I mean by breaking down a number of different scenarios.

In both business and athletics, I had responsibilities for personnel, budgets, revenue generation, expense control, and results. The one area that was closely related between business and athletics was personnel, so let's start with that.

Managing People

"I know God will not give me anything I can't handle. I just wish He didn't trust me so much." (St. Mother Teresa, Roman Catholic nun who devoted her life to serving the poor and destitute)

In business you're in charge and have authority over your workforce. In some cases you are required to recruit for those positions, but in large companies this task is assigned to the Human Resources Department. Likewise, in some cases you are in charge of employee development, but in larger companies, again this task is left up to HR.

In small college coaching you're in charge of and have authority over your staff (if you have one) and your players. Since your staff consists of possibly only one or two assistant coaches or grad assistants, let's equate a business's employees instead to an athletic team's players.

I feel there are two major differences between managing employees and coaching players. The first difference is age. Employees normally range from 18 to 65 years of age, whereas players normally range from 18 to 22. This is a huge difference, which I will expound upon shortly. The second big difference is turnover. In business, employee turnover ranges from 1 to 10%, unless you happen to be managing something like a call center or a restaurant, where the numbers would be higher. In college athletics, you are looking at theoretically on average a 25% turnover each year. This, therefore, is a significant difference between business management and college coaching and is addressed in the next chapter.

Age Differences

Addressing the first difference, i.e., age, you almost have to experience it to believe it. Eighteen vs twenty-two in itself is an enormous difference in maturity levels, and it's a real challenge to assimilate a whole new set of 18-year-olds into your "Workforce" every September. Some are mature - most are not. For many, if not all of them, this is their first time away from home for an extended period of time. It's the first time they do not have a parent / guardian "supervising" them 24-7. It's the first time they are "free" to do whatever they want, whenever they want. Unlike a manager, who strives to make the eighteen-year-old productive over an eight-hour workday, a coach must be concerned and involved in an 18-year old's entire day. Guidelines need to be established that assist the young man in eating right, getting proper sleep, studying, and sometimes even socializing - all over and above assimilating them into a team environment and helping them become productive members of that team. A coach's job is not over when the workday practice ends. Therefore, a coach has to have in place a plan/strategy to make all of these things happen. Many coaches establish procedures whereby they are notified by a professor if a player misses a class or fails to turn in an assignment. Many also establish an evening study hall, supervised by an assistant coach. At bigger schools, athletes have a training table that caters to the needs of strenuous athletic activity. Some coaches have a curfew. All of these may work - but all require resources, mainly personnel resources. If you don't have the resources, which many small colleges do not, then your only recourse is to do this all yourself or establish a culture where the upperclassmen "adopt" the cubs and lead and nurture them into successful behavior patterns. In addition, you need an educational program that teaches the pathway to success in the areas of body strength and quickness (weightlifting, plyometrics), body health (sleep, nutrition), academic success (study habits, testing aids), and I also included spiritual health (prayer, Bible study).

There is a great divide between business and sports as it concerns the age of the employee/player, in my opinion. College basketball is dealing with young, sometimes immature players, and business is dealing with more mature and experienced employees.

At BC, since we did not have a strength coach, nutritionist, or spiritual director for the basketball program, I created a program for each. Because my appointment wasn't effective until mid-August, the first year was simply a learning experience for me in these areas. I learned what was available, and what was not. I found out that the football team had an assistant coach who was dedicated to weightlifting training for the football team only. None of the other 15 sports had a weightlifting trainer. I learned that the college had two nurses work part-time dealing with students who are sick, but there was no nutritionist on campus. I learned that the college had an academic assistance office that provided academic guidance and student tutors when necessary for the student body (about 750 kids in 1998-99). I learned that the college had one chaplain to provide spiritual guidance to the entire student body. Basically, I learned that if I wanted any of these things for the basketball team, I was going to have to develop a program to incorporate these things into my daily routines. So, my second year I started that process.

These are things that few in business have to deal with in supervising a workforce.

Attitude Development

I actually used the same model in both business and coaching to try to influence attitudes. I had been using the 3F Model for Success (**Exhibit 3**) at SW Bell and decided that it fit well with where I wanted the players to go when it came to overall attitudes. I had created the model while working on my doctorate and copyrighted it in 1997. The 3 F's were Faith, Family, and Fitness, in that order. Fitness was further broken down into spiritual, mental, and physical. **Exhibit 3A** at the end of the book describes exactly how the model is defined, but a "quick & dirty" summary would be:

- Faith – putting God first in all you do
- Family – taking care of one another
- Fitness – being healthy

- o Spiritually, Mentally, Physically: in order to achieve, you must learn how and then practice what you learn

Along with the 3F Model came my Management Creed. It is found in the bottom half of **Exhibit 3**. It includes 13 things that I personally believe about people, processes, and how people want to be treated:

- Each person wants to do their best.
- People will perform at peak levels if they are doing what they really want to do in life.
- People like being told (often & sincerely) that they do good work and are appreciated.
- Partnerships win.
- The "S" in success stands for "Sacrifice."
- Only dumb luck can beat working hard and working "smart."
- Proper planning and organizing build the foundation for attainment.
- The ability to communicate and the commitment to do so are vital to efficiency and effectiveness.
- Everyone must be a leader. Everyone must be a follower. Wisdom is knowing when to play which role.
- Leaders remove roadblocks and keep their group focused.
- Lessons learned from small failures pay big dividends.
- What goes around, comes around.
- In your retirement years, what will really count is the number of friendships you have cultivated, not the number of promotions you received.

I tried my best to follow these 13 points when I was a manager at SW Bell, and I continued to do so after I arrived at BC.

One of the first things that was covered with all new recruits the first day they arrived on campus was the 3F Model for Success and my Management Creed. I always arranged for a meeting with all new players on that first day, and the first thing I covered were these two items. I felt that it was important that they know my philosophy (which I would have already covered with them in the recruiting process – see "Mission & Goals" below) and were given an opportunity to adopt the model for themselves, if they so chose. (Frankly, I don't know if any did adopt them, although I do know that an alum from

Nebraska who was a banker adopted it for his bank when he saw it in our annual basketball brochure.)

Now looking at the Model you can easily see that it could be used in many different settings, be it business, sports, politics, etc. But most interesting to me is that the Creed appears to have been almost designed for a team sports setting. I did not do this on purpose when I created it, but I'm sure my athletic experiences, coupled with my business experiences, led me to glean from those experiences those major concepts that led to success and satisfaction.

I continued to use this model and creed all twelve years I coached at BC, and I still stand by them today.

There are two other items that I used to help form the proper attitude: Our Mission & Goals Statements, and a program I called "In Pursuit of Excellence" which I introduced to the team in about my 8th year at the helm. (**Exhibits 4 and 5**, respectively)

Mission & Goals

The mission of the Benedictine College Men's Basketball Program is to win a third NAIA National Championship, while developing young men into leaders who will make this world a better place in which to live.

- *Our goals are simple: to win games on the court, and to change hearts off of the court.*
    - *Integrity, aspiration, resilience, determination, and a Christian love for others create the foundation for achieving these goals.*

As a program, we will make the maximum effort to achieve our mission.

I introduced this mission and these goals to my first team at BC and every other team I coached during my tenure. I covered it with potential recruits and their parents and stressed it in pre-season meetings with players and coaches. I tried to live by example through hard work and trying to exemplify the virtues espoused in the goals section. We never did accomplish the goal of winning a third National title. Only time will tell if we achieved the goal of making the world a better place in which to live.

"In Pursuit of Excellence"

After having established a set of mores during my initial years at BC, a number of which are described in sections below, I decided somewhere around my eighth or ninth year to formally implement a program that allowed each player to document their plan to achieve excellence in academic, athletic, spiritual and social pursuits.

The document I provided to them is shown in **Exhibit 6**. It broke down each respective area into a goals section and a plan on how they were going to achieve the goal. The team goal in each area was provided for them, and they were to figure out how their personal goals could lead us to successfully accomplish each respective team goal. I spent time in pre-season, shortly after they arrived on campus in August, going over the document and providing guidance to each player and assisting them in documenting achievable methods that would allow them to be successful. Each player turned in a copy to me for a final review. Periodically during the school year, we would assess how well we were doing. (It didn't matter if you were a JV player or a varsity player – this program was meant for all team members.)

Fr. Hugh giving post-moves advice to 6'8" Jim Losev

This was the final piece I had developed for attempting to shape the right attitude within the program.

Summarizing the difference in this attitude development scenario for business vs. athletics, I was able to use the Mission and Goals, the 3F Model for Success, and the JB Creed in both settings with comparable success.

Spiritual Development

One of the first things I remember doing and probably the most important one was to approach an old Benedictine monk friend of mine, Father Hugh Keefer, and ask him if he would consider being the men's basketball team's chaplain. I knew Fr. Hugh very well when I was a student and we had kept that relationship alive for over 30 years. While I was in school, Fr. Hugh was extremely active with the student body. He knew most of the 1000 guys who attended Saint Benedict's and could be found daily beating one of them in handball up in the old gym. (I made the mistake once of saying racquetball, and he quickly and firmly corrected me - handball was for men; racquetball was for "others.") When I returned to campus in 1998, I found that Hugh was totally disconnected from the college. He was working as the assistant manager in the Abbey's business office, and that vivacious spirit I knew back in the late 60s was gone. When I asked him to consider being our chaplain, he told me he'd think and pray about it and talk to the Abbot before making a decision. Hugh took about a week to decide, and thankfully he said yes. He also made it perfectly clear that he would not only show up for home games, but he planned to be involved in our daily routines also - and he was. Once a month he said a team Mass, where he kindly was able to make the non-Catholic players feel welcomed and included. He taught them to cross their arms as they approached him when he was distributing communion to the Catholic kids, and he would give the non-Catholic players a blessing instead. It was the players' option to approach the altar and receive this blessing, and it was really heart-warming to see every player do that at every Mass he said for us over the years.

This man in his seventies came to every practice. He was at every home game and said a prayer with us on the bus prior to every road game. Most of our road games were on the radio, but if they weren't, he expected a phone call as soon as the game ended. I still remember our conversation prior to our first home game his first year. He asked me where he should sit - in the stands behind the team or on the bench? I told him I wanted him at the end of our bench praying for our success. I also told him that if things got really bad, "you and I will switch positions." You had to know Hugh, who was a master at needling people. There were a number of times over the years

106

when things weren't going so well on the court and he would meander his way over to my chair and say "Is it time to switch yet?"

One additional comment on Father Hugh - he became a revitalized man. He became the old Father Hugh I knew in school. He became close to many of the players - he was like a grandfather to them - and he was very popular with the players' girlfriends and mothers. He was definitely a "charmer."

Comparing the spiritual development scenario between business and athletics, I find a serious difference. It was easy to pursue this goal at a Catholic college like Benedictine – not so much in the business environment. I did try to model spirituality at Bell, but you really had to be careful that you didn't overstep your bounds. The furthest I went was to read from the bible the Nativity story at my organization's Christmas luncheon. I'm not sure you could even think about doing that in today's business environment. I'm sure it would "offend" someone. So from a spiritual development scenario, there is no similarity between business and athletics. In fact, I'm not sure just how much spiritual development could be pursued at a non-religious college, so spiritual development may only be achievable in specific college athletic situations, unfortunately.

Academic Development
Having the spiritual issue resolved, I next had to turn to the academic issue.

I personally had learned a system of studying while in high school from Father John Hiltz, a great English teacher. His system of text reading and note-taking had benefited me all the way through my doctoral degree. (All my friends will tell you it certainly wasn't my intellect that got me through.) I decided to teach the system to all of our players. So, every August, after the new recruits arrived, we would have a "Fr. Hiltz training class", and I would go through a detailed example of how to read a chapter, highlight the important points, and set up a review schedule of notes and highlighted texts. I'd also teach them how to take notes during a lecture, how to summarize those notes, what to highlight from the notes taken, and then how to review your notes prior to an exam. The final item I taught them in the August meeting was "Time Management." This may be the most important lesson you can teach a new college student. Most failures, in my opinion, don't come from a lack of intelligence but from lack of good time management. I'll never know how many of our players implemented this system, but I guarantee you those that did got good grades and graduated. (**Exhibit 7** is the Time Management and Study Techniques handout I provided to the players and **Exhibits 8 and 9** are the items I covered with them on Study Techniques and Test-Taking Tips, respectively.)

In addition to the lesson on reading and note-taking, I also established a study hall for all incoming players and for any returning players who had less than a 3.0 GPA. This study hall was set up in the late afternoon on days we practiced at night, and after dinner on days when we practiced in the afternoon. The study hall was monitored by our seniors, who were expected to be role models for the underclassmen.

The third thing I did was to provide detailed information on the academic Assistance Center provided by the college. This group provided tutors, study guides, and test-taking instructions for our students at the college. This was the third leg of the stool that provided the academic piece of our "Success" system.

There are similarities in both business and athletic scenarios for academic development. In business you create budgets and make plans for developing your subordinates, be it in some type of management training or technical schooling. You analyze what your needs are going to be from a personnel expertise standpoint and then schedule the proper training for the effected employees. So there is a connection between business and athletics for academic development pursuits.

Physical Development

The next item I tackled was the physical development piece. Personally, I had worked out practically daily since graduating from college, and at 50 I was in pretty good shape. However, the predominance of my strength training came from using Nautilus machines. I knew most, if not all, college programs used free weights or a combination of free weights and machines to physically develop their players. My first problem was that BC did not have any Nautilus type machines. A second problem was that the weight room was located at the football complex, which is about a quarter of a mile up the hill from the gym, and which the football team had first dibs. (That normally wouldn't be a huge problem, except at BC the football team had 180+ players. There simply wasn't much time outside of class time for any of the other 15 varsity sports teams to lift.) The third problem was that we did not have access to a weight training coach.

I was able to resolve the first problem by raising enough money to take advantage of a Nautilus program that gave schools a very good price on used Nautilus equipment. We bought 11 really nice units from Nautilus and put them in the "student workout room" just above the offices in the gym. (The room consisted of four treadmills - 3 were broken, a rowing machine, and three or four stationary bikes.) This allowed me at least to get a novice lifting program going for the team. The second thing I did was talk to the football coach and find out when the open times were for lifting at the football complex. I scheduled our team for three times per week in the open slots, regardless of the time, be it early in the morning or late at night.

The last task was for me to bone up on weight training for basketball athletes.

For this research I used what at the time was available on the internet and the library and talked to my sons who had participated in lifting programs as invited walk-ons while at Nebraska and K-State. I tried to find training videos on free weights, and most importantly, talked to a good friend and former Raven football All-American, Keith Hertling, who owned a couple gyms called "Popeyes" in the Topeka and Kansas City area. From all of this research I created a lifting schedule for the team (**Exhibit 10**). (Weightlifting was certainly needed - we had a 6'8" 215-pound forward who could not bench press 105 lbs.!)

Again, this is an area where little commonality exists between business and athletics. The closest business comes to addressing physical development is from an "Employee Benefits" perspective. Some companies will have (as part of their health plan) free or reduced-price club memberships so that employees will exercise and maintain better health. Business does this for two reasons; first, so that people are healthy and are on the job every day, thus cutting back on absenteeism, and secondly, to reduce the costs of the company's health care plan. The fewer claims, the less the cost to the company through its healthcare vendor.

Even though business may address this in some fashion via their "Wellness Program", the reasons are substantially different. In athletics, physical development is pursued so that the player can perform at his/her peak. In business it's to save the cost of health premiums and to reduce the costs of absenteeism.

Nutritional Development

Finally, it was time to tackle the nutrition issue.

I talked to the cafeteria manager, who was a really good person, about setting up a training table for athletes. He was sympathetic to the cause, but really did not have the staff or budget to prepare meals for anyone other than the student body. So, my task then became how to educate our players to eat right. Based on their size and calorie burn daily, what and how much should they eat and drink. Again, I did research similar to the weight training research and created some nutrition charts which allowed the players to calculate their own dietary needs. (These charts were part of a 29-slide PowerPoint presentation I created to teach them about nutrition in general. **Exhibit 11** is an example of one of the charts they used to calculate their overall calorie need each day.) To be honest, I don't know how many, if any, actually implemented a plan. I had the same experience concerning sleeping habits of my players – I really didn't know how many were getting the number of hours of sleep required to be effective as a college athlete. There were some things, frankly, that you had to trust that your athletes would take to heart simply because they wanted to get better.

Comparing business to athletics, nutritional development also falls into the category of "not so much." Some progressive companies (like Google) may provide a nutritional option for in-house meals, but most do not. What and where you eat is your business, and the company does not get involved in these decisions.

Summary

These are some of the issues faced by college coaches based on a "workforce" of 18 to 22-year olds that are not faced too often by business managers. Some of topics could be loosely related to a business entity's orientation program or its health benefits package (Wellness Program), but most are not applicable to business. From reviewing Attitude, Spiritual, Academic, Physical and Nutritional Development, Attitude and Academic development are about the only ones that lends themselves somewhat to both business and athletics, in my opinion.

Business Cycle vs. Academic/Sports Cycle

"Having a blank slate is sometimes as daunting as it is exciting." (Joe Madureira, American comic book writer/artist and game developer)

One thing that was extremely refreshing in college sports, which is drastically different than in business, is the fact that you get to start over at the beginning of every new Academic Year. Regardless of how good or bad the previous year may have been, there always seems to be a sense of positive anticipation on the part of the coaching staff and the players come September of each new academic year. Unlike business, where every January your books started over but your circumstances were the same as they were on December 31st, in academic sports all records are 0-0 and almost always the players have changed. It creates this annual optimism that is contagious. This is somewhat true for the fans, but inherently ingrained into the fabric of college coaches. Unlike business, where the players (employees) do not change from year to year unless you bring in a new management team, college basketball loses the previous year's seniors and sometimes some underclassmen and replaces them with new recruits. The fact that your slate is wiped clean leads you to believe that your team's results will improve from the previous year's record in most cases. As I had said at the beginning of the section, it is refreshing to get a chance to start over with a clean slate and a new set of players. And the cool thing is that all schools are in the same boat. Everyone loses seniors and recruits new players. Plus, again unlike business, you can change your strategy based on your player personnel changes. A number of times we went from one season to the next and significantly changed our strategy. The strategic decision was based on the type of players you had in a specific year. Whatever best fit their offensive and defensive skill sets determined what type of offense or defense we were going to implement that year. If your school is really good and you have the proper resources, you can develop a strategy that works well and then recruit players who fit that strategy. However, we did not have that luxury. We had to take the best player available and then mold our strategy around our collective players' skill sets. In business, changing strategy is rare, and is normally only done when new management takes over, or when previous results are bad, and a major overhaul is required. That then eliminates this annual "Re-genesis" found in college athletics, mainly due to the fact that strategies and players (employees) remain somewhat constant. And in academia, it is not only true in sports, it's also true in the classroom. Each year you have a new set of students who contain different skill sets than the previous year's class. It is refreshing.

Example: One year I had 10 players of almost equal ability, and remarkably, we had two players at each of the five positions on the court that were equally talented. It's great to have depth, but it is also difficult to find enough minutes in a 40-minute game to go around for 10 players. Amazingly the skill sets of the players allowed me to break them up into two groups who played totally different styles. One group, made up mostly of white players, were good at playing a deliberate, pattern style of offense. On defense, they played a great matchup zone. I called them my black team. The second group, made up mainly of black players, were very athletic and excelled at pushing the ball on offense and being aggressive to the basket. On defense, they picked up in a full court press, and played a Run and Jump style of defense putting pressure on the ball regardless of where it was on the court. I called them my white team. We played 5 in + 5 out, with each group playing five hard minutes at a time. Preparing to play us had to be somewhat of a nightmare for opponents, for they basically had to come up with 2 game plans, not one. Interestingly, John Calipari at Kentucky used this system a few years ago and did extremely well. I'm sure he probably reviewed some of our 2005 game films in preparation for his season that year!

The cycles for business and college sports/academics, differ drastically, as outlined above. (My good friend, Bill Toepfer, says he still remembers the first day of class in grade school – "new classmates, new Big Chief tablet, new box of crayons [loved the smell}, new pencils with erasers still intact. It was a new adventure each year.") It is too bad you can't have a "re-set" each year in business – it sure boosts the energy levels.

So, You Want to Be a Coach ... Lesson #7A:
Have a plan even before you take the "Dream Job" as to just how far you will go and how much time you will spend developing the "whole person" versus simply developing that person's sport's skill set.

So, You Want to Be a Coach ... Lesson #7B:
Know and understand the particular circadian rhythm of the sport, and its environment, in which you will be coaching.

Chapter 8: Comparing a CEO to a Coach

"The first responsibility of a leader is to define reality. The last is to say Thank You. In between, the leader is a servant." (Max Depree, American Businessman and Writer)

A number of years ago I read a best seller business management book by Patrick Lencioni entitled *The Five Temptations of a CEO*. I thought the book not only interesting but also perceptive in breaking down those traits (temptations) that derail leaders from being successful. I thought I'd use Lencioni's "temptations" as a way of measuring my performance as a coach to see if I personally fell into the pitfalls that he outlined in his book, and thereby provide anecdotal evidence that the two professions are practically twins (or maybe only distant relatives). Simultaneously, I thought I'd also provide my opinion on being able to use these five "temptations" to analyze, in general, the equivalence of being a coach versus being a CEO.

Lencioni's five temptations are:

1. Choosing status over results
    a. Becoming more interested in protecting your career status than making sure your company achieves results
2. Choosing popularity over accountability
    a. Not telling employees what is expected of them and reminding them of those expectations consistently, and when performance is not up to expected levels, dealing with it directly and professionally, and not worrying about being "liked"
3. Choosing certainty over clarity
    a. Ensuring your decisions are correct; being absolutely sure of something before making a decision and thus keeping employees in the dark
4. Choosing harmony over conflict
    a. in decision making, discouraging or not allowing productive ideological conflict (Can't we all just get along?)

5. Choosing invulnerability over trust
    a. pretending to be perfect instead of being open to others' ideas and input and thus gaining their respect and honesty.

Choosing Status Over Results

"The very purpose of existence is to reconcile the glaring opinion we hold of ourselves with the appalling things that other people think about us."
(Quentin Crisp, an English writer and actor)

Ego may drive most coaches who are pursuing coaching as a profession or a career, but it wasn't a factor in my situation. In my case, after retiring from a very good corporate position, my only desire was to bring national recognition/respect back to my alma mater's basketball program. I didn't care if I got coach of the year in the league (which I didn't) or in the nation. As long as our team was successful in becoming a national force to be reckoned with, I would have been happy and satisfied. We flirted with it, but never really got there and stayed there. (Ranked 10th in the nation in NAIA D2 in 2007 and 14th in the nation in NAIA D1 in 2010.)

I don't believe this "temptation" (*Becoming more interested in protecting your career status than making sure your company achieves results*) is much of a factor in any coach's success/failure. A coach may have an ego and seek status, but what most colleges are looking for is someone who can win at their school. In order to be a candidate for these types of jobs, in almost all cases the coach will have to have had positive results (winning record) at another school. The one thing about the coaching profession that is so different than business is that your results are public – they are out there for everyone to see. Your record is published and historically documented, so there is no way that you can fool a new employer by claiming success on your resume that isn't backed up by your actual record. Therefore, I don't think this first point from Lencioni's list is applicable when comparing a coach to a CEO.

Having said that, I do believe that after achieving success (winning) at an institution, a coach could fall prey to this "temptation" by letting that success go to his/her head. Ego can really get in the way of future success, and, like many other professions, thinking you are better than you really are leads to certain failure.

A coach also may be tempted to water down his non-conference schedule so that the appearance of success (20-win season?) is not reflective of actual success against comparable competition. How many times have you been involved in a discussion about teams who have won 20 games but were not chosen in the field of 68 for the NCAA tournament? Just look at teams from the power conferences just prior to the start of their league season. How many are 12-2 or 13-1 but end up 20-12 overall? From appearances it looks like good results, but is 7-11 in the league really success? In this case, Lencioni's first temptation just may be applicable.

BC knocks off another tough team

By HANK LAYTON
hanklayton@npgco.com
Atchison GLOBE

Coming into this season, Benedictine College's early schedule looked gloomy.

A 51-45 win over No. 19-ranked Columbia College on Tuesday — along with wins over Northwestern University, Rockhurst and College of the Ozarks to start the season — certainly brightens things up.

"I like this group, and they're having fun," said BC head coach Joe Brickner, whose squad also almost beat Cardinal Stritch — a team that nearly knocked off NCAA Div. I Wisconsin-Milwaukee.

College of the Ozarks was the NAIA Div. II runner-up in the national championship, and Rockhurst is an NCAA Div. II school.

The Ravens (4-1) got their latest win Tuesday against the NAIA Div. I national runner-up thanks to defense, highlighted by eight blocks by junior big man Chris Bonham.

"We had a little session yesterday because of what we did Saturday," said Brickner, whose team gave up 90 points in the loss to Cardinal Stritch. "Nobody was ever in stance, so we had a little heart-to-heart as a team and decided we're going to play a little defense the way we know how."

Please see KNOCKS/Page 13

HANK LAYTON/Atchison Globe

Benedictine College junior Kristian Williams (12) dishes the ball with a Columbia defender at his feet during Tuesday's win.

(However, looking at this from the other perspective as it pertains to my philosophy at BC, could I personally have "balanced" our non-conference schedule and played only half as many "higher level" teams? Our records would probably have been better, satisfying the fans and the administration. We would not have had as much in "game fees" paid to us, which would have limited the speed of making the physical and program improvements that were made, but maybe the players would have learned the lessons necessary from the tough competition and gained confidence from playing other teams that we could beat. This is definitely a question that begs asking.)

Choosing Popularity Over Accountability

"To his dog, every man is Napoleon; hence the constant popularity of dogs."
(Aldous Huxley, English writer and philosopher)

This is an interesting temptation to analyze (*Not telling employees what is expected of them, reminding them of those expectations consistently, and when performance is not up to expected levels, dealing with it directly and professionally, and not worrying about being "liked"*). I like when people like me. I don't do things that aren't "me" in order for someone to like me, but I'd much rather have a friendly relationship than an adversarial one. That was true with the players as well as it was with my assistant coaches. I do think, though, that I held them accountable for what was expected of them in their role, with one exception. I had a former player who became my graduate assistant and eventually my assistant coach. In my attempt to groom him for my position, there were times that I would do work that an assistant should do while he was doing "head coach" work.

Quite often I would take the scout team and teach them the opponent's offense and defense while Coach Peer, my young assistant, worked at the other end of the court with the first and second teams going over offensive adjustments I had devised from watching film of the opponent's defense. In hindsight, in my attempt to maximize the value of the information gained from scouting the opponent and simultaneously groom Coach Peer, I may have inadvertently programmed the players to subconsciously think of him more as a head coach and me as an assistant coach. Most head coaches would have sent the assistant to work with the scout team and the head coach would work with his top ten. I had confidence that Coach Peer would do a good job with the top ten while gaining valuable experience as "the one in charge." I knew, and he knew, that the buck stopped with me, and that I called the shots. That is all that mattered to me, but it may have caused doubt or a lack of confidence in my ability to coach from a player's perspective.

I was pretty strict on holding the players accountable for their physical condition, their "team" attitude, their skill development, their effort in practice and in games, their academic standing, and their social behavior. I made things clear upfront and reminded the players often of these things. When someone violated the rules, they were held accountable by me. I tried to do that for all players, not just those who weren't as talented.

One year I even went so far as not allowing my most talented player to play his senior year due to his lack of accountability. Interestingly, the year he did not play, we had our best record in my 12-year tenure. I knew he wouldn't like me, but I thought by allowing him to keep his scholarship, but not play, he would learn the lesson that you have to use your God-given talents to their potential if you truly want to be successful in your life. Basketball was his life, and not being allowed to play his senior year was difficult. However, he returned his senior year and a fifth year in order to get his hours to graduate.

I personally don't think this temptation has much application in the coaching ranks, although I have not been around other college coaching environments to make a good assessment. Most coaches, I believe, hold their staff and players accountable, since results are directly affected. And in coaching, without positive results, you get fired.

Choosing Certainty Over Clarity

"I used to think I was indecisive, but now I'm not too sure." (Anonymous)

This temptation (*Ensuring your decisions are correct; being absolutely sure of something before making a decision and thus keeping employees in the dark*) is not too applicable to the coaching profession, in that you don't have time to get all the information necessary in order to make a "safe" decision. Game time does not wait, so you decide how to play a game with the information you have, and you decide during the game what to do again with the information that you have. There is no waiting for better information.

How this temptation may apply, though, is from a scheduling perspective (playing a "safe" schedule).

> My vision that I conveyed to the team was that we were to become a small college basketball power. In order to do that, I always scheduled an extremely difficult non-conference season. We would play anybody, anywhere. Of our 10 to 12 non-conference games each year, only 2 or 3 were at home. Up to half of our games would be against teams with more scholarships and much bigger budgets than ours. The remainder was normally against some of the top NAIA Division 2 teams in the country. I wanted our players to be tough. I wanted them to respect our opponents, but never to fear them. I wanted them to go into a tough conference game against a top ranked opponent and know that they had already played teams

117

that were bigger, stronger and quicker. I wanted them to have confidence in their ability to beat good teams on the road. Now this was a dangerous strategy. I could easily have been setting my teams up for failure. It is very difficult to beat good teams on their home court, especially if they have more resources (scholarships, budgets, and recruiting bases) than you. I was also pretty much guaranteeing that we would lose at least 10 games each year even if we were successful within our league. However, the record was not too important to me. Beating good teams and advancing to the national tournament was important. And once you get to a national tournament, the playing field gets a lot more level. The favored teams aren't playing on their home court, they do not have officials who may tend to favor them, and the pressure is on them. I have seen it so many times in my personal basketball career – a team with a poorer record, but tough-tested players, simply "mans-up" and wins. That is what I wanted our kids to experience.

Many coaches do not take this approach. They play a soft non-conference schedule so that their record is a good one and it reflects on them as having been a good coach. No one remembers after the season is over as to who you played – they just remember the record. If you can win 20 games in a basketball season, you are considered a good coach by most observers. They never take the time to research who you beat and who you didn't beat.

I can relate this "scheduling" scenario as an example of the 3rd temptation. I don't think I fit in that category because I chose for my teams to get better by playing higher level competition rather than worrying about the team's overall record.

Choosing Harmony Over Conflict

"We sleep in separate rooms, we have dinner apart, we take separate vacations – we're doing everything we can to keep our marriage together." (Rodney Dangerfield, American comedian)

Most coaches will tell you that team harmony is a key to team success. I would agree with that assessment. The harmony Lencioni refers to has nothing to do with team harmony, but rather assistant coaches' harmony (*in decision making, discouraging or not allowing productive ideological conflict*).

I made sure from the start that my assistants knew they had the authority to challenge my strategy and tactics. However, it had to be behind closed doors.

Conflict among boss and subordinate is healthy if it is private and it gets all the options out on the table. (For a good training film on what could happen when you don't speak up when you disagree, try to find an old video of "*The Abilene Paradox.*") Better decisions are made when all the options are analyzed. Once they are analyzed and a decision is made, however, loyalty takes over. There can be no second guessing the boss by a subordinate in front of others. Seasoned coaches like Chic Downing, Mike Martin and Joe Huber, who helped me in my first few years, understood this concept. They were basically volunteer coaches, and each one was excellent in their own way. All had been successful head coaches previously, so they fully understood the role of an assistant and how valuable a good assistant coach was to a program. I had occasions later, however, where due to the inexperience of an assistant, he would challenge/attempt to correct me in front of the players. In some minor instances, this is okay. For example, if I were to say pre-game meal is at 4 pm when it actually was set up for 5 pm, then it is the responsibility of the subordinate to say something. However, if at practice I describe a strategy that we were going to follow in defending a certain team and the assistant disagrees with me in front of the troops, there is a problem. The players must believe the coaching staff is on the same page. If they don't, some will follow the head coach, while some others will follow the assistant. This creates chaos and ultimately disaster.

As it concerns team harmony, this has more to do with team dynamics than Lencioni's 4th temptation. Team harmony will occur if everyone on the team accepts the role he/she has been asked to play in order for the overall strategy to be successful, as was discussed in an earlier chapter. That doesn't mean there won't be disagreements. It does mean that those disagreements will be addressed by the team and a resolution will be found based on the overall strategy of the team and the roles each individual has been asked to play in order to achieve that strategy.

Choosing Invulnerability Over Trust

"To make mistakes is human. To blame someone else for your problem, is strategic." (Anonymous)

This temptation (*pretending to be perfect instead of being open to others' ideas and input and thus gaining their respect and honesty*) is applicable to coaching. The stereo-typical coach is one who lives by mantra "It's my way or the highway."

How often have you heard a coach say, "You aren't paid to think – you do what I tell you" when a player makes a mistake and when asked by the coaching staff how he could have done such a thing, the player begins with a response "I thought …"? Our image of a good coach is one who doesn't make mistakes. He/she is all-knowing, all-calculating, all-wise. Here's a tip for you – that's a bunch of crap! Coaches make mistakes all the time. Some are man enough to admit it – in front of their team – and some are not. I didn't seem to have that problem, probably due to my corporate upbringing. In corporate America, you make small mistakes all the time. In fact, that is one way to make progress – small mistakes. You must learn from each small mistake and not allow it to become a big mistake, but trial and error is a way of life in business. The same is true in coaching. Owning up to a tactical error in front of your players is not a sign of weakness. It is a strength that will allow them to see that you, too, are human. What they also will observe, though, is how you learned or recovered from the mistake. If it spawned a subsequent success, the incident will solidify your credentials and gain their respect.

There were a number of times where I had to admit that I made a wrong decision in front of my coaching staff and my players after a lost game. Very seldom is one error going to lose the game, just like very seldom is one player's mistake going to lose a game. But it will be a contributing factor. I always felt that if I did make a mistake and owned up to it, we grew closer together as a team. They could see that I was vulnerable, and it helped them gain a certain amount of trust in me. If I could trust them to execute on the court the way we executed in practice, even though they made mistakes, they could trust that I would make a good decision a high percentage of the time, even though periodically I would error also. The key was for all of us to learn and improve from the mistakes – to grow – together.

Summary

So, overall, there are some similarities between being a CEO compared to a coach. I'd rate the relationship as being maybe first or second cousins. The similarities, in my opinion, hover around the principle of how you treat others. Is there a mutual respect shown in how you relate to your employees/players? Do you "walk your talk"? Where I think there is a separation comes from the perspective that in most cases the coach has more authority and control than a CEO. (An outlier here for the coach is today's use of social media – but that is a whole new discussion topic.) Part of that has to do with the size of the organization - a coach is dealing with 15 – 25 players and assistant coaches, whereas a CEO is usually in charge of a large number of employees, many with which he/she does not have daily contact or a direct personal relationship. In other words, the characteristics of leadership are similar, but its application differs significantly, in my opinion.

As far as the ultimate judge of the CEO's success is concerned, according to Lencioni, it is dictated by the results on the bottom line. In business that is usually measured by Stock Price, Return on Equity (ROE), Market Share, Economic Value Added (EVA), or some similar numerical statistic. In coaching, success is most likely interpreted to mean wins versus losses. In that case, I was not a success. My overall record was below .500. Lencioni goes on to state that "this is not to suggest that other "human" factors are not important, or even most important, on a spiritual or emotional level. But the one in charge, the CEO (Coach), is ultimately responsible for the results of the company (team), and this must be his final measure."

Discussing "Walking your talk" with good friend Delbert DeWitty at Retirement Party.

So, You Want to Be a Coach … Lesson #8:
Don't think that since you were a good CEO (or business manager) that you will automatically make a good coach.

Chapter 9: How It Ended

"Everything that can be counted does not necessarily count; everything that counts cannot necessarily be counted." (Albert Einstein, German-born physicist who developed the special and general theories of relativity)

The end of my tenure as BC's basketball coach may have come as a surprise to many connected to the college, but my wife and I knew it was a possibility a year earlier. In my end-of-season meeting with the President and AD in 2008-09, I was given an ultimatum – either make the national tournament in 2009-10 or you will be fired. (Remember, the last time a BC team made it the national tournament was my senior year, 39 years earlier.) I did not like the ultimatum, not because they were frustrated with the program not making it, which I shared in the frustration, but rather because I finally felt we had the tools to recruit the type of player that would get us there. (See **Exhibit 12** for the 9-page analysis I provided to the President and AD at the end of the 2007-08 season. It listed the things required, in my opinion, to make BC a winner in men's basketball. Some of my recommendations were implemented in my last two years, but most weren't implemented until after I left the program.) We were getting 8 scholarships in 2009-10 and 9 scholarships the next year and could reduce the squad size to 15 players, a far cry from the 6 scholarships that had to be spread out over 24 players that we lived with for 10 of my 12 years at BC. I could pay for recruits' visits now for the first time. Our campus, due to the leadership of the president, had been transformed from a 750-student campus to a beautifully developed 2000-student campus. I had nurtured a set of consistent donors who allowed us to have a budget that was adequate to run a program. With the administration allowing me to reduce the squad size to 15 from 24, now we were only coaching players capable of playing at the college varsity level – no more JV for enrollment purposes. There were so many good things that finally had become available, and it bothered me that now that these things were available, I only had one year to make them pay off. But bottom line was, I had not led us to the national tournament in 11 years. Twelve was the number that would break the camel's back.

Even though our record ended up 16-14 in 2009-10, we almost pulled off what everyone thought was impossible. In late January, we were 13-4 overall and in second place in the league at 6-2. We were ranked 14th in the nation - and rightfully so – we had beaten two of the three NCAA D2 schools we played in regular season games, we had beaten the national runners-up for both NAIA D1 and D2, we had beaten the better teams in the league so far that season, and simply put, we were pretty doggone good. Then the bottom fell out – all four of our big men (2 starters and their backups) were either injured or sick from Feb. 1 on. Without a front line, we simply couldn't win, losing 7 of our last 8.

Two days after the end of the 2009-10 season I was asked to come to the president's office for a meeting concerning an eligibility issue I had challenged in December.

I had a 6'9", 250 lb. transfer student who was not eligible first semester according to NAIA rules. In order to be eligible the second semester, the NAIA required that his overall GPA, including all the classes he took at all colleges, be a 2.0 {C average}. When I turned in the eligibility roster for second semester in mid-December, even though his overall GPA was a 2.1, the Academic Dean told me the player would not be eligible. When I asked why, I was told that the college, 2 years earlier, had implemented a rule over and above the NAIA rule which required the student to have a 2.0 his first semester at BC. This young man got a 1.7 and was therefore ineligible. The rule was news to me – I'm not sure why I was not aware of the college implementing something that would affect transfer students, since this rule affected basketball more so than any other sport. [We were the only sport who carried over from one semester to the next.] I immediately asked for a meeting between me, the Dean, the AD and the President. I did not feel like this was a fair rule, for transferring to a new school can be difficult, and it may take time to adjust academically. I proposed that we implement the stricter rule after two semesters, not one, so that the transfer could become acclimated to the academic expectations of the college. [My recommendation seemed much more reasonable and fairer to the student-athlete. Plus, I really needed for this young man to be able to play – I had been playing our 6-10 center, who had bad knees, for about 34 minutes per game. He had been terrific so far, but it was only a matter of time before his knees would give out if he continued to play so many minutes each game. (In January and February he could not practice with us due to the pain in his knees. He only participated in games.) In addition, the 6-9 freshman that I had signed to back-up our 6-10 center, who was going to be a very good player, broke his

123

leg before the season started and was out for the entire year.] Even though I had repeatedly asked for this meeting through not only the Dean, but also the AD and the President from mid-December through February, it was not scheduled until early March, two days after our season ended.

At the meeting were the head coaches of football, baseball and basketball, plus the Dean, the AD and the President. After some discussion, the group agreed that my proposed change made more common sense, and it was adopted immediately. {Unfortunately, it was too late to be of any benefit to my team – had it been changed in December as I had requested, or even January, our season could have been drastically altered.}

After the meeting ended, the President and AD asked me to stay for a few minutes for a subsequent meeting. I knew what the meeting would be about, and I knew what the outcome would be. As I suspected, I was asked to resign. I refused. (I never quit until a job is finished. Never have, and never will.) When I refused, I was informed that I was fired. I was offered a full-time professor's position in the Business department if I wanted to stay, but my coaching days were over. I told the two of them that I would have to take some time to decide if I wanted to stay and teach or not, and the President agreed to give me time to make the decision.

Since there had been a small group of alums working with the president and the AD on a replacement for me even before the season was over, it was only a matter of few weeks before a new coach was hired.

The Last Day

"Success is how high you bounce when you hit bottom." (General George Patton, regarded as one of the most successful United States field commanders of any war)

What started out as my second-last day at BC actually ended up being my last day. I had anticipated that it would take two days to clean out my office and get everything ready for the coach who was replacing me, but as it turned out, a little overtime allowed me to finish the job and the job to finish me, so to speak, in one day. Here is how it unfolded:

Since Easter was approaching, I decided to go to Confession at our parish church on the Monday before Easter. The Assistant Pastor, "Fr. Riley", volunteered to hear confessions between the 6:25 a.m. Mass and the 8:15 a.m. Mass on Mondays each week. Since I really enjoy starting the day with the peacefulness of Mass, I decided to go a little early that day and go to confession before the 8:15 Mass. The line was about 10 deep when I got there, but since it was only about 7:10 a.m. I knew I'd eventually get to go to confession before the priest had to leave to say the 8:15 a.m. Mass. Since I had some time before it was my turn in the "hot box", I decided to review a pamphlet that was in the vestibule that guided people through the process of making a good confession. I seem to always confess the same type of sins, so I thought that maybe I was forgetting some things and this pamphlet just might jog my memory for things that should be confessed and weren't being recalled. The pamphlet followed the Ten Commandments for the most part, expanding upon them so that under things like "Thou Shall Not Kill" you would find things like "Have I inflicted another person with verbal or emotional abuse?" After reviewing the more than 100 items listed, I still only had two things that I thought I needed to confess. Not that I'm a goody-two-shoes, but since I got fired, I didn't have the energy to sin. When it came my turn, I went into the confessional and confessed my sins. To my surprise, for the first time since I can remember, the priest started quizzing me for additional sins! He asked if I had been eating or drinking too much - I said "no." He asked if I had stolen anything – I said "no." It seemed like everyone in authority was questioning my skill level – the president and the AD doubting my coaching ability and the priest questioning my ability to examine my own conscience.

After Mass I drove the hour to Atchison to start what I thought was my second-last day on the job. I played ball in the gym with the local "noon-ballers" from town and then had lunch with a very good friend at the local Chinese buffet (Oh no! Gluttony?) When I went back to my office to box everything up, I didn't get too far. A few of my players stopped by to see how I was doing, and I visited with my assistant coach and other staff and faculty who stopped by to visit.

One of the reasons I chose to clean out my office on Monday was because a press conference had been scheduled for Tuesday to introduce the new men's basketball coach. (The 11 a.m. press conference was to introduce a "big-time hire," according to the AD's press release, and the AD was arranging for the cheerleaders, the band, and local dignitaries to be there as well as giving door prizes for students who attended.) The AD had asked me to clean out everything so that the new coach could move in the week following the press conference. I figured that I could get most things cleaned out Monday when the new coach was not around, and then come back later in the week and finish while he was attending the Final Four in Indianapolis. The President had also planned to have a big welcoming party Monday evening for the new coach and his wife at the President's home, which was located on campus at the northeast corner of the College's entrance. The athletic department and the infamous local "dignitaries" were invited, so it was supposed to be a big deal. In fact, the AD sent out a notice to the invitees (which I was one since my name was still on the athletic secretary's email distribution list) telling them to come meet, as the AD called him in the invitation, "the big-time hire" and his wife. The party started at 8 p.m., so I thought I would still be okay since I thought I'd leave campus long before then.

I started packing everything around 3 p.m., starting with my national championship plaque and the two frames that held a copy Dr. Naismith's original basketball rules, including his handwritten corrections. (This was a gift from a fellow professor at BC, Dr. John Settich, who knew Dr. Naismith's grandson. The grandson had signed the copies.) As I progressed, the time got later and later. One of my strengths (and sometimes weaknesses) is that once I start something, I won't quit until I'm finished. Well, it got me that day. The time became 7 p.m., then 8 p.m., then 9 p.m. – when I finally had everything cleaned out and packed up, it was 9:30 p.m. I removed the name plate from my door, gave one last look at my "cleaned out" office, turned off the light and closed the door. It was my final goodbye.

It took me four trips to my pick-up truck to load the boxes of items I had removed from my office. As I slammed the tailgate shut and got in to drive away, I drove along the side of the gym. In a flash my mind raced with all the times that the ball didn't bounce our way, all the poor calls officials made, the apathy of the student body even when we were winning...and suddenly I found myself flipping the bird to the gym! I never use that gesture – ever. But there I was driving along the sidewalk flipping the bird at Nolan Gymnasium. Then I started laughing – at myself. Here was a 61-year-old man using a teenage gesture aimed at an inanimate object. I bet Fr. Riley will love hearing that during next month's confession!

That was not the end, though. I still had to drive out the entrance to Second St. to head home. Yes, you guessed it – I had to drive right by the President's house, where the "big-time hire" was meeting and greeting the "dignitaries." (Don't misinterpret me – I liked the new coach and I respected him. He was a very good coach and I expected him to do well – I just found the terms "big-time hire" and small college basketball to be fundamentally opposed.) As I drove west out along the entrance, I looked to the right and saw through the large glass window of the lower section of the President's house a man standing with his back to the window as if he was addressing a group. I couldn't tell if it was the new coach or the President. I only glanced for a moment – but for a second, I started feeling sorry for myself. Here I was, after having given all of myself for twelve years to the school and the basketball program, driving my red 1997 Ford Ranger pick-up (with all my memorabilia in the back) out of the campus for the last time. There was no fanfare, no one to even say goodbye – while simultaneously viewing the celebration of someone who was going to take everything that I had built and use it to further his career. However, as I turned left out of the entrance onto Second St., what came to mind was Jesus' story of the Prodigal Son. I remembered the older brother saying to his father, "Here I am, your son who has toiled and been faithful to you for all these years, and you haven't given me as much as a young goat, so I could celebrate with my friends." And the father responded saying, "Everything I have is yours." In that moment I realized that this wasn't about me. This was about Benedictine College Basketball. The Ravens were once the pride of small college basketball. I gave 12 years of my life to rebuild it. It was now at a point where it had become nationally competitive once more and what I had contributed was now the foundation for someone else to build onto to regain our position of prominence. Yes, it was a time to celebrate – I had done my job, and it was now time for the new coach to do his. Fr. Riley would have been proud of me.

So, You Want to Be a Coach … Lesson #9:

In the coaching profession, getting fired is something that happens often to the good and the bad. Don't take it too seriously; remember when it does happen, take the high road.

Chapter 10: Saying Goodbye

"I have fought the good fight, I have finished the race, I have kept the faith."
(2 Timothy 4:7)

Bringing my tenure to an appropriate closure was a goal of mine, seeing as the Administration decided to keep me out of any basketball affairs after informing me that my contract would not be renewed. I decided to have an end of year banquet for the team at one of their favorite local restaurants. I told them that they could bring a date as well as their parents, and I invited a few people who were close to the program via working at games, etc. to join us. Since we had recruited nationally, there were only a few parents who could attend, and about half the team brought dates.

The Last Function

"How lucky I am to have something that makes saying goodbye so hard."
(A.A. Milne, English author best known for the Winnie-the-Pooh books)

I felt it would be important to close this chapter of my life not only for my mental health, but also for the team so that they could move on and transfer their loyalties to the new coach and not feel guilty. We hosted the dinner at Cedar Ridge Restaurant, which is a converted barn literally out in the middle of nowhere. I am serious when I say that if you didn't have a map, you couldn't find the place – and still, it was always packed. The proprietors believed in serving very good food (family style) at very reasonable prices and serving it with great Midwestern hospitality. The place was a favorite of our team, and it was the only place I considered when I decided to have a final banquet.

Setting the Table

"The secret to success is constancy of purpose." (Benjamin Disraeli, former prime minister of the United Kingdom)

Most of the guests arrived by 7 p.m. for the start of the banquet, except for the team itself. Since there was a bridge out, the detour and the back way to

Juco transfer Alex Miller had a terrific season going before getting sick

Benedictine College's Alex Miller (22) puts in two of his 15 first-half points during his team's 92-8... ...merica Nazarene Thursday.

get there were both serpentine routes that required a guide. It was bad enough trying to find the place when the bridge was functional, but finding it now was about as easy as finding the motive behind a politician proposing a solution to a problem that is actually in the people's interest! When the team finally made it around 7:30 p.m., the kitchen was ready to start serving so we didn't have a lot of time to visit other than to say hello. I asked everyone to be seated at the various tables around the private back room, and then joined my wife and her family at a table near the entrance. The food was great, as was the

company. After the peach cobbler alamode was served, I stood up and addressed the room. I decided to break the comments into two pieces – one addressed the current year's results, and the

Abby, Jeremy and Noelana enjoying the team's last get-together.

second addressed the progress made over the last 12 years. It was easy to talk about this team's success – in just our second year of moving into the NAIA D1 category, before sickness and injuries set in late in the season, we had climbed to 14th in the NAIA Division 1 national rankings. It was the first time the school had been ranked in the NAIA D1 poll since I played for the Ravens in the late 60's. I congratulated the players who earned all-conference honors, and those who ended up ranked in the top 10 in the country in individual statistics. I also ran through the numerous stats that the team had accumulated that placed them in the top 15 in the country in certain specific statistics. I wasn't trying to blow my own horn (He who sings his own praise is usually off key!), but rather I was trying to remind these young men that they had had a successful year. Without the injuries and illnesses at the end, we easily could have won 20 games and been in a great position to earn a spot in the national tournament. I really felt it was important that they carry forward the attitude that they were a good team and had a bright future.

The second portion of my comments were directed at the way things were when I arrived, and, due to the generosity of friends, family and alums - plus some hard work, the way things were now as the baton was passed. (**See Exhibit 13.**)

I painted the picture for them of what it was like being a recruit 12 years ago and what they would have found back then. It was a drastic difference from today. I wanted them to realize that compared to what I found when I arrived, the program was now a first-class operation when compared to our competition. The point I tried to drive home to these young men was that after they get their degree and become successful, it is their responsibility to "give back" to the program. Without the financial backing I received from friends, family and alumni, none of those physical things that made it a first-class program would have been possible. Funding the program is critical to its success and they needed to carry on the legacy.

Regrets

"It is the things that I might have said that fester." (Clarence Dane, pseudonym of Winifred Ashton, an English novelist and playwright.)

I then moved on to the regrets, highlights, and cherished memories over my 12-year tenure. Among the regrets was failing to reach the national tournament, especially when we were so close in 2003 and 2007. However, my biggest regret was that I never was able to convince a whole team to buy in to what it really meant to be a "Raven."

My memory of being a player at St. Benedict's was that we were the toughest, mentally and physically, of any small college team in the nation. You walked with a swagger, but if I can describe it as such, it was a humble swagger. We worked hard, bought in to the coaches' system, and did the right things on and off of the court. We had a "refuse to lose" attitude, and nothing was more important to our team (and the student body) than winning basketball games. And we won a lot. That toughness, willingness to sacrifice, and putting the team first attitude was something I talked about practically every day to our teams in one way or another, but it never seemed to take root. The 2002-03 team and this final year's team came the closest to gaining these attributes, but didn't quite get there. I could never figure out

Back in the Day.

exactly why I couldn't succeed in teaching them these principles – maybe I recruited the wrong type of player; maybe I did not communicate the concepts effectively; maybe today's athlete has too many options and distractions to care about these principles and the reward for buying in is not worth it. As I get away from coaching for a while, I hope I can identify the reason for my failure. I may find that it is as simple as the fact that our college, and life as a college student-athlete, has changed very drastically since I was a student. St. Benedict's was an all-guys school, a mini-Notre Dame if you will, only with basketball as the identifying sport instead of football. Benedictine is now co-ed. During my time as a student-athlete, St. Benedict's did not have football – only soccer, basketball and baseball. Benedictine now had 16 sports teams, diluting the importance and popularity of any one sport significantly. In my day we did not have ESPN – we learned about the great teams and the great players by reading articles in books, magazines, and newspapers which seemed to emphasize the finer qualities of team-oriented athletes. Today you have the sports media glamorizing the individual and his or her accomplishments, followed up more often than not by the athlete himself espousing how great he is. Times certainly have changed, and without a large staff monitoring every athlete's waking hour, it seems much more difficult today to influence the athlete to do the right thing. Not that all the athletes are this way – every team I had had a few players who bought in. The problem was getting ALL the players on the team to buy in.

Highlights

"You measure the size of the accomplishment by the obstacles you have to overcome to reach your goals." (Booker T. Washington, born a slave on a Virginia farm and became one of the most influential African American intellectuals of the late 19th century.)

Among the highlights of my coaching career were the times we beat the No. 1 ranked team in the nation when no one thought we had a chance. It happened in

2000-01 when we beat the two-time defending NAIA D1 national champions (Life University) at McKendree University's Classic, and then again in 2007-08 when we beat the defending NAIA D2 national champion (MidAmerica Nazarene University)

on our home court. Other highlights were the first-year turnaround in

Benedictine's record (from 5-26 to 17-17 overall and 0-18 to 9-9 in the league) even though I only had time to recruit one player for that returning team; beating two out of three NCAA D2 teams in my final year; and helping a high school back-up center, Dan VanDyke, become an NAIA All-American in 2007-08, the school's first All-American since 1972. My most cherished memory, though, was the relationships I developed with my players, especially those who did buy in to the principles of toughness, selflessness, loyalty, and hard work. They were not my most talented players, for the most part, but they were ones who would dive for a loose ball not only in a game, but also in practice. They were names some wouldn't recognize or remember – but I always will. They were "Ravens."

The Future

"Our deeds determine us, as much as we determine our deeds." (George Eliot, pen name for Mary Ann Evans, an English novelist, poet, journalist, translator)

The final topic I addressed was the future.

I told them that I had accepted a position in the School of Business as an Associate Professor, working mostly with graduate students. However, for the next year or so I would be on campus at least twice a week teaching the Capstone course for undergraduate business majors, so I would be able to see them periodically and keep up with what was going on in their lives and the lives of their families. As for their future, I told them that it was bright. I made sure they understood that the new coach was a very good one. He would, though, have different processes, rules and teaching methods than what they had been accustomed to with me. I strongly encouraged them to buy in to his system and do whatever he asked of them. I also told them that they needed to work hard between now and next season to get better personally. Unless they improved individually, the team would not improve.

Closure

"Don't cry because it's over; smile because it happened." (Dr. Seuss, pen name
for Theodor Seuss Geisel, an American children's author, political cartoonist,
and animator.)

With the final subject covered, I felt that closure was at hand.

I decided to end my reign the same way we began each practice and ended
each game, with the team's prayer, the Our Father. Before each practice we
would gather in a circle at half-court and hold hands. I'd say a short prayer
and then we all would recite the Our Father. (With the H1N1 virus – Swine
Flu - running rampant my last year, we decided to go fist to fist in a circle
instead of holding hands so that we minimized the possible exposure of
transmitting a virus from one to another.) I used this technique for three
reasons; first, so that these young men saw that it was okay for a man to
pray, and to do so in public without being embarrassed; secondly, to ask for
God's help in accomplishing our goals; and thirdly to signify that we were one
(a connected circle) and only by working as one could we be successful.

It seemed appropriate that ending the banquet saying the Our Father would bring
an end to 12 years of seeking God's help in accomplishing what He sent me to
Atchison to do. When I told the group that I would like to end with the Our
Father, it was really cool in that my team immediately stood up and grabbed the
hand of the person next to them. The room was way too small to make a circle,
so the unbroken string of clenched hands meandered its way in and out of tables
and walkways. I said, "We are one", and then began the Our Father. As everyone
joined in, I struggled to say the rest of the words out loud. Choking with emotion,
I knew this was the final verse that closed my 12-year book of love.

So, You Want to Be a Coach … Lesson #10:
*Build relationships as you progress in your tenure; you will cherish them long
after that tenure ends.*

Chapter 11: An Epiphany

"After crosses and losses, men grow humbler and wiser." (Ben Franklin, American Founding Father)

My belief prior to becoming a college coach was that a good coach could win a lot of games, even if his team's talent level is less than the opponent's - if his players played hard, smart, and team basketball. After 12 years of experiencing "less talented teams" than many of our opponents at BC, I came to the conclusion that I was wrong. Sure, there are times and games that you beat a more talented team, but at the college level, the coaching is solid, and most games come down to whose players make plays.

We had one year at BC where we had probably as good of a starting 5 as anyone in the conference. We placed 3rd out of eleven teams that year. (Unfortunately, only the top two teams went to the national tournament.) We started the year very slowly, going 1-5 in early non-conference games trying to use a sophomore and a freshman at point guard. The other four positions were seniors (two of them 5th year seniors due to injury red-shirt years the

Seniors Marx, Peer, Carrington, Henningsen & McGowan

season before), and all four were good players. (All scored more than 1000 points each in their careers.) I decided that I had to have senior leadership at the point, so I moved our shooting guard to point, handed him the ball and said, "You've got to run this team." He did a terrific job, sacrificing his scoring in order to lead the team and help us focus and execute on both ends of the floor. We won six in a row after that and ended up going 19-13 overall and 15-5 in the league. It was a good year, but it could have been a great year. All five league losses came down to the last possession. In four of the five, we had the last shot. In all four, we executed the play exactly as it was drawn up. Unfortunately, all four shots misfired. In the other loss, our opponent had the last shot and hit it. My wife never understood me when I used to say that

"Players make plays." I can't count the number of times that teams I played on went down the stretch in a close game and someone would step up and make a play and we'd win the game. It might be a jump shot, a layup, a free throw, a blocked shot, a defensive steal – one of us would do something that allowed us to win. "Players make plays." It's a mindset. It's a toughness. It's a part of your will that won't allow you to lose. I was blessed to play with people like that in college and on the AAU circuit after college. It drove me crazy that I could not teach it, and apparently could not recruit it as a college coach. (Don't misunderstand me – I am not blaming the lack of crunch time players for our lack of success. The kids played hard and tried to win. They wanted to hit that last shot or make that late steal. But the only one who came close to a "players make plays" candidate was an overachieving guard from KC who hit two game winning jumpers on plays designed for him in the huddle.)

What is bizarre is that I was able to "recruit" or develop people like that in business. You know them – they are the ones who nail the report the day before it is due or sway the client to continue to do business with you even though the competition has lower pricing. Why could I not do that with these young men? I never did figure that out, and it frustrates me to this very day. And I'll go to my grave wondering why we couldn't have hit just one shot, or got one stop, when we needed it most in the big games.

Self-Evaluation

"Without proper self-evaluation, failure is inevitable." (John Wooden, College Basketball Coach)

Overall, I believe I was a decent coach. We were extremely organized, and always well prepared for what our next opponent was a good at, and where their weaknesses were. Our game plans attempted to exploit their weaknesses and take advantage of our strengths. We practiced hard, and we were in better physical condition than most, if not all, of our opponents. My game plan always came down to us executing better than whomever we were playing. I depended upon our defense being so good that we could have an off day shooting and still win. Looking back on it, we sure did have some bad shooting days!!

I was okay at making in game adjustments but could have certainly gained vital experience learning this skill had I had a few years of being an assistant to a head coach who was good at doing this, someone like a Larry Brown. It's funny how you know how to do this when you are on the court in the point guard position, but standing on the sidelines is such a different perspective. I think I got caught up in watching specific situations in a game and did not always have the bigger perspective in mind. Also, I got way too involved in worrying about how well the officials were doing (normally not so good, in my opinion.) and did not focus enough on what we had to do to counter things that our opponents were doing that we had not seen on film. Obviously, as I grew in experience, I got better at all of these things. But it sure would have been nice to sit on Bill Self's or Hubie Brown's bench for a year. Watching them perform and learning what worked and what didn't, from strategy to working with officials, would have benefited someone like me tremendously.

What I was good at was determining matchups. I guess I had seen so many players over my playing years that I got a great feel for what it takes to negate a player's strengths and exploit his weaknesses. I was much better at this if I had an opportunity to watch a player live rather than just on film.

I remember the first year I was at BC; we had beaten the No. 2 team on the road in the league playoffs and had to go to the No. 3 finisher for the league tournament semi-finals.

Talking adjustments during a time out.

They had beaten us pretty handily once and won a close game the second time we played them in the regular season. They had a 6'6" forward whose job was to sprint down the court on defensive rebounds and station himself in the corner. His teammates would pitch ahead to him in the corner, and he would lace a three. In both of our losses he was effective, and our 6'6" forward seldom made it back to cover him in time. So, for the playoffs, I put our 5'6" point guard on him. Our players thought I had lost my mind. They were convinced that the 6'6" kid would kill our point guard and that he would simply post him

138

up and score at will. However, in two games I had not seen this kid make a good post up move. In addition, our players, including the point guard, thought the 6'6" opponent would simply shoot over him whenever he caught the ball. But I had noticed that this kid would bring the ball up from his hip as he shot, so our guard could easily prevent this. In fact, our PG could pick him if he tried it, because the ball was out in front of the player's belt as he rose up to shoot. I then took our 6'6" forward and had him guard their point guard. Again, I had noticed that their point guard was a facilitator, not a scorer, and especially not an outside shooter. I just told our forward to deny any dribble penetration, which our forward could do because he was pretty quick laterally.

The opposing coach (Larry Holley, a NAIA Hall-of-Fame coach at William Jewell College) probably wondered what the heck was going on after the opening tip and when he saw the matchups. The 6'6" opponent, as I had suspected, was not open in transition like he had been in previous games, because our point guard was back with him to deny any pass. We did not have to scramble to adjust defensively after Jewell crossed half court, because the point guard stayed on their forward and our forward picked up their point guard. And also, as I had suspected, their forward only tried to post up once in the first half and was unsuccessful because if he put the ball on the floor, it was ours due to the quickness of our point guard, and if he turned to score, he was facing three somewhat athletic 6'6" Ravens there to help.

Well at halftime we were down 1, and their forward had zero threes and, I believe, two points. Our game plan was working, and we were in excellent position to take this down to the wire. We changed nothing at halftime in the locker room. When the second half started, William Jewell scored the first 11 points, nine of which came from their 3-point shooting forward. I had called time-out to try to slow their run and find out what we were not doing that we had been doing in the first half. I made it a habit to ask players in the huddle "What do you see?", for they may be seeing something that I am not. No one came forward with any observations. Well, we played them evenly the rest of the game, but ended a season that had some great late season possibilities with a 10-point loss on the road. It was really disheartening, for we were playing some of the best basketball in the league at the end of the season.

After the game was over, I allowed the seniors to go home with their parents if the parents were in attendance. The rest of the team dragged themselves onto the bus for a ride to the local fast food joint and then the hour ride home. When we got out of the restaurant and were heading home, one of the 6'6" juniors on the team came to the front of the bus with another junior forward. They wanted to know if I knew that after halftime our two senior guards and our 6'6" senior forward got together and on their own decided to switch back and guard a player their size and abandon our game plan matchups. The point guard went back to guarding the point guard, and the forward went back to guarding the 3-point shooting forward. That explained why the shooter got 3 3-point baskets in the first 90 seconds of the second half. Needless to say, I was extremely disappointed in the behavior of these seniors. (These are the same guys who went 5-26 (0-18 in the league) the year before.) I really thought they had become believers – but I was wrong. The only positive that I thought came out of the situation was that my juniors, now seniors to be, realized that maybe the coaching staff knew a little bit more than they had been given credit for, and the following year's team would have senior leadership committed to following game plans.

I think of how I would have handled such a situation in business. I would have probably fired the three individuals responsible for the "mutiny." In my more than thirty years in business, I don't recall anything like this ever happening. That is not to say it didn't – it may have, and I may have never known. But what it did for me at BC was to confirm what I had thought when I first got there – "these folks don't know how to win." They had become so comfortable losing, that having the discipline and trust that it takes to win was non-existent. This had to change, and it was not going to be easy because the acceptance of losing had become ingrained into the program. As I once told a close friend, my first years at BC we had the best drinking team in the nation. (Don't misunderstand me – these were not bad kids. They were good kids who learned bad habits.) I probably should have cleaned house when I got there, but I did not. There were a number of players on this team that did not fit in that category, but it takes a whole year or more to learn that most players aren't willing to do what is necessary to win. By not cleaning house, I had freshmen, sophomores and juniors who believed losing was just fine, as long as the gals noticed you and you could party after the games. That was what was important – not sacrificing to win. Driving that attitude out of the program took me about 6 years. There were a couple of kids already there and there were some kids we recruited who were winners. They did all they could to win. Unfortunately, with limited scholarships, we simply did not have enough of the "new blood" to eradicate the "old blood."

As a side note, about 7 or 8 years after graduating, I received an email from the point guard who was involved in the change in game plan scheme. He had become a high school coach in St. Louis, had married, and had children. His note to me was to thank me for teaching him leadership, discipline, and a will to win. I was pretty surprised when I received his note. He said little things that I had done, like the John Wooden "how to put on your socks and shoes" routine, had really made a long-term impression on him. He said at the time when I taught them how put on their two pairs of socks and how to lace up and tie their shoes, he thought I was silly. However, after he got out of college and got into the real world, he realized that it's the disciplined little things that allow us to be disciplined and thorough in the bigger things. You don't know how much it means to a coach to know that he has touched the lives of his former players in a positive way. The point guard's note helped remove some of the sting of the "mutiny" I had felt years earlier. (Also, I kept up with what was going on in the life of one of the other two players involved in the incident, and he has turned out to be a terrific dad and husband, and has had a very good career up to this point.)

As I Was Saying...

"Hard work beats talent when talent fails to work hard." (Kevin Durant, American professional basketball player)

Going back to my original point – I was wrong thinking that a good coach could consistently beat teams who were more talented. I had mentioned Larry Holley earlier. Larry won the league title numerous times, was the coach of the year in the league multiple times, and almost always finished in the top 3 in the league. He had a great program going in our conference. He had been at William Jewell for over 30 years. He had a great summer camp program where he could literally start recruiting kids when they were in grade school. He recruited predominantly in the KC area, so his players could work his camp in the summer and play every night after camp against other college players back home for the summer. He could offer a kid the same scholarship as we did but convince the player to stay at home instead of the dorm, and the cost of attending a private college just got $8K to $10K less than going to our school. He was a very good recruiter who had his tentacles woven throughout the western Missouri and eastern Kansas. (Shoot, he'd have 5 assistant coaches sitting on his bench at games!) And he knew how to coach. His teams were always well prepared, executed well, and played hard. (They were also the best at holding on defense without being caught.)

Prior to my last year coaching at BC, Larry's school announced they were going NCAA Div. 2 in two years. It wasn't something Larry necessarily wanted to do, but the school thought the NCAA moniker would be a recruiting benefit for regular students. So, two years later William Jewell College joined one of the best NCAA D2 conferences in the nation. (Fortunately for Jewell, the eastern division had the top NCAA Schools, and the western division, other than Drury University in Springfield, had teams that were less competitive at the national level. Jewell was in the western division.)

Larry was now facing a different animal. He was competing with schools who had been NCAA D2 for a while, so their talent level was a notch above his. Also, he would have to play the eastern division once each year, which almost certainly meant 6 or 7 league losses. But Larry Holley had over 800 college wins. If he was that good, shouldn't he be able to make Jewell a winner at the NCAA D2 level? Well, history did not bear that out. He had one .500 season or better overall, and his league record was not good. Does this mean he was no longer a good coach? Not by any means. He was a terrific coach – but he didn't have the resources to compete at the new level. He didn't have players who could make plays at that level. His KC connections weren't producing the talent he needed to win, and when it did, the kids played a year or two for him and then transferred to what they perceived to be a better D2 program. My point is – my original perception of being able to coach less talented teams to consistent victories over more talented teams is an anomaly. You've got to have the players to win consistently at the college level.

In business it is somewhat the same. As Jim Collins says in "Good to Great", you've got to have the right people on the bus and those people have to be in the right seats.

So, You Want to Be a Coach … Lesson #11:

Simply strive every day to do your best.

Chapter 12: 20-20 Hindsight

"The grand instructor, time." (Edmund Burke, Irish philosopher and statesman considered the father of modern conservatism)

Here I am sitting on the North Carolina beach in Salter Path reminiscing about my coaching career and what effect it had on me and what effect I had on those I touched while coaching. As I write this, it's been 9 years since I last coached a college game. Time has healed some wounds and softened others. Scar tissue, however, still exists from not getting a chance to benefit from the changes I had recommended but were not made until about the time I left. I still feel like the president stole my dream from me right before it came to fruition. Many fired coaches probably feel the same way. It's both comforting and hurtful to know that the program was able to make the National Tournament the third year after I left. The additional scholarships, the additional budget, the allowance of reimbursing recruits for public transportation, the further development of my assistant coach, the fact that two of the best teams in the league left and went to NCAA division 2, plus the league getting three automatic bids to the national tournament instead of two - all of these, I'm sure, contributed to BC earning a spot in the National tourney. Add to this the following items and you had a formula for success.

- the recruiting experience of the head coach who was hired a year after I left (the coach who replaced me left after his first year there when he realized the recruiting methods he was able to use at previous NAIA schools was not going to work at BC, nor be accepted by the administration)
- the new recruits brought in
- the coaching experience of the new head coach
- the added support from the administration

What If? And What Really Is Success Anyway?

"Success has nothing to do with what you gain in life or accomplish for yourself. It's what you do for others." (Danny Thomas, American nightclub comedian, singer, actor, producer, and philanthropist)

Would we have reached the national tourney had I stayed? We'll never know. What I do know is that the four sophomores who were in my top six players my last year at BC beat the University of Missouri Kansas City, an NCAA Division 1 school, when they were seniors. Does it matter that we never made the National Tournament while I coached? Probably not to anyone but me. My passion was to lead a team on to the same court in Kansas City some 40-plus years after I had done the same thing as a player in 1970. We were so close a number of times, only to fall short. One of my first questions to God when (if?) I get to heaven (God's mercy willing) will be "Why could you not allow us to qualify - even once?" I'm sure his answer will make sense when looking at the big picture.

Dear Friends Mary & Bill Toepfer

My very good friend, Bill Toepfer, tells me I should consider my coaching time at BC a considerable success. He says my influence on all the players who came through the program will be much more profound than any won/loss record. My wife has said the same thing many times, but she almost has to say that! My friend, who has known me as a close friend for over 45 years, knows and has been a part of my business and athletic success during many of those years. He shares my disdain for losing, my desire to do it the right way, my belief in always giving my best effort and to never give up. He says these are things that have been ingrained in my players and they have taken these values and made them part of their lives. I hope he is right. For those players I have been able to stay in touch with, many have successful families and careers going for them. But there are many players who I have lost track of - are they also successful husbands, fathers, breadwinners, and spiritual leaders? I pray for them often, and hope God has them in his protective embrace.

145

Do-Overs Anyone?

"When you look back on anything in life, hindsight being 20/20, some things you'd have like to have done differently." (Stone Cold Steve Austin, American retired professional wrestler, actor, producer, and television host)

So, sitting here on this beautiful evening on the white sands of North Carolina watching the waves, I ask myself "What would you do differently if you could do it all over again? "In a perfect world, I would live in Atchison instead of Kansas City. We chose to live in KC because either myself or my wife would have to make a long drive to work, and we felt it was better that I drive instead of her. The one-hour drive to and from school over 12 years took its toll on me physically. It also limited my ability to nurture local relationships, monitor players, and respond to issues that required me to make a quick trip to campus.

Secondly, I would have infiltrated the Kansas City High School coaching ranks. Recruiting is 80% of the college success algorithm, in my opinion. I needed to carve out time to create relationships with the Kansas City High School coaches so that we had an opportunity to sign some of their talented players.

Third, I would have signed more shooters and played the ones more that I had signed who could shoot. Because we played a pressure man-to-man defense most years, I leaned toward recruiting more athletic players. There are a lot of good shooters who aren't athletic. The three-point shot has changed the game, and trading 3 for 2 isn't a bad strategy, especially when your talent level is somewhat less than the competition's.

Fourth, I would have raised more money so that I could have sent my assistant coach on the road to scout and recruit (bought him a reliable car??). Since there were twenty-four small colleges and an additional 20-plus jucos in Kansas, there probably wasn't a high school game played in the area where there weren't at least three or four assistant coaches there recruiting. The few games I was personally able to attend found me in a line of up to 10 college-level coaches standing in the hallway outside the locker rooms waiting to talk to a potential recruit, "usually the same kid." In most cases, however, we weren't there, and I found in recruiting that players and parents notice who is coming to watch them play. Over the course of the season a relationship is created which weighs heavily in the decision process of a recruit. So many times we had to start the process late, sometimes after the high school season ended due to our lack of funds and personnel. This created a real disadvantage for us with the local recruits. One of the main reasons we were successful in Arizona is because coach Van (who was getting paid nothing) would target his top choices early in the season and then go to as many of their games as possible. He thereby created a relationship with the family, which gave us an advantage and at least got them to visit our campus. The other disadvantage we faced was the story that jucos and NCAA D2 schools were telling the recruits. The D2 schools would get marginal D2 level players to "walk on" by glamorizing NCAA versus NAIA, and then making sure the parents knew it would be cheaper to walk on at their school

Coach Van with Service Award

than it would be to get a scholarship from an NAIA school (most of which are private schools) and have to pay the difference between the scholarship amount and the full cost of attending the NAIA school. Unfortunately for us, the latter statement was true. I could offer a full tuition scholarship ($16,000 when I started, $24,000 my last year), and the kids could go to Pittsburg State as a walk-on for $8000 total and pay less than our room, board and fees ($10,000)! I can't tell you how many recruits we lost to jucos and D2 schools based solely on these recruiting pitches.

The jucos were much worse. If you weren't aware of it, practically every High School starter thinks he's D1 material, or at least NCAA D2. His AAU coach and sometimes his parents reinforce this false belief. Regrettably they do not have a clue as to how good you have to be to get a D1 scholarship. The jucos were notorious for leveraging this false belief. They would tell a kid "come play for us, and in two years you'll be signing with an NCAA D1 school." That simply was not true. The fact is that if a D1 is not interested in you in high school, they will not be interested in you 95% of the time out of juco. What jucos were not telling these kids was this, "We can have five or six out-of-state players on our roster. They are the ones who are going to get to play. The remaining players must be in-state players, and you would be a good candidate to fill one of these slots for us. You won't play much, many of your courses will not transfer to a 4-year school, and two years from now you're going to have to start all over socially, basketball-wise, and academically. But hey, 14 years ago we had a Kansas kid sign at Podunk State (a small D1), and you can do it too!"

As I had mentioned earlier, invariably, 2 years after a recruit enrolled at a Juco or an NCAA D2 school, they would be calling wanting to transfer. In most cases, we were not interested anymore, since he already burned two years of eligibility and many of their courses would not transfer to our school. If we signed them, it would take 3 years to graduate, so we would be giving up an additional year's scholarship and getting little, if anything, for it.

Final Do-Over Questions
> *"Fear regret more than failure" (Taryn Rose, an orthopedic surgeon turned shoe designer and serial entrepreneur)*

The final 20-20 hindsight question to be asked is "Knowing what you know today, if you could go back to 1998 would you make the same decision you did then and leave corporate America to coach college basketball at Benedictine College?" It is so hard to give that question a "yes" or "no" answer. Below are some reasons why.

Job Perspective
Not knowing what would have happened with SW Bell is one factor. I was not happy in the IT job I was performing in

Swapping the SBC hat for the BC hat

1998, and only the Good Lord knows how long I would have been in that position, or any position with Bell at the time. The "family" business culture had changed at Bell, and the only thing that seemed to matter to the leadership was quarterly financial results. We were losing our "service first" mantra, and employees were looked at more from a numbers perspective as opposed to a valued asset. Those employees with long service records and valuable experience and knowledge were being forced or enticed out of the business and being replaced by younger, cheaper labor, if they were replaced at all. I could have very easily been one of the casualties as time moved on.

On the other hand, with SBC (SW Bell's owner) buying up a number of other "Baby Bells", there certainly could have been other non-IT opportunities for me had I patiently waited for one to present itself. (When I retired in 1998, SBC was ranked #9 on the Fortune 500 list.) Had I stayed at Bell in a job I enjoyed, my financial situation would have certainly been better today than if I left. Connie and I would have probably had to move a couple more times, most likely to San Antonio and then to Dallas. We were not opposed to moving, since we did not have family in St. Louis and had enjoyed our visits to San Antonio in the past. Many of our Bell friends were already located in San Antonio, so moving there would have been rather easy socially.

From a job perspective, there is no comparison about the satisfaction you get from coaching versus being in a corporate position that is not in your wheelhouse. So, even though we would have done much better financially staying with Bell (I think), the nod goes to the coaching position from a job perspective.

Basketball Program Perspective

Looking at this from the perspective of the Benedictine Basketball Program, would they have hired someone who would have done a better job and had a better record than me? Possibly. The huge task facing the new hire in 1998 was "how do you repair a program that had literally crumbled over a 25-year period?" The program's record had not only declined significantly, but in addition the program's assets and resources were practically zero. I have chronicled in other parts of this book what a sorry state practically everything was in at the time. The only thing going for the new hire would have been the new gym built in 1996 (although it was designed more like a high school gym than a college facility) and a new apartment style dorm for seniors that had been refurbished from the old Abbey building (Freshman Hall) which had been boarded up for over 30 years. (It had not been torn down previously only because the college did not have the funds to pay for its demolition.)

> I still remember the first day on the job at BC when I entered my "tomb" office. I found, literally, an inch of dirt under a throw carpet (not a throw rug – it was a piece of carpet cut down to a rug size). The desk was so old that when you opened a drawer, you could not place anything in it, because none

of the drawers had a bottom in it. The chair would give a young person osteoporosis, and the file cabinets were metal ones that were rejected by the armed services in World War I. There were no windows in the tomb, and if you left your door open to try to get some heat into the tomb, the likelihood of a volleyball rocketing across your desk was about 100%. The second day I was on the job I brought in a nice rug from home, my computer and computer hutch from home, and replaced some of the file cabinets with ones I had at home, and got a new chair.

Rebuilding the infrastructure of the program was going to take a lot of money and a lot of time. That does not mean that the team's record wouldn't have improved significantly without these resources – as in business, there are "quick fixes" out there.

Graceland University (IA), a member of the Heart of America Athletic Conference (HAAC), did just that a couple of years ago. Graceland had been a perennial bottom feeder in the league until they brought in a juco coach who had done extremely well in the juco post season tournament the previous year. He brought the core of his juco team with him, and his second year at Graceland his team won the NAIA Division 1 national championship! They didn't win the league title either year he was there, but they qualified for the tournament his second year and rode a hot streak in the tournament all the way to the crown. That coach left Graceland after the championship for a NCAA D2 job, and the following year Graceland was right back to where they had been in the league for years. I don't know if he improved any internal processes during his short tenure, but my guess is that he didn't. Quick fixes, again like in business, seldom improve long term, consistent results.

BC needed more than a quick fix, in my opinion. They needed someone who could not only turn the record around, but also rebuild the infrastructure, re-establish a winning mind-set, and stabilize a program so that if that coach left, the next coach could hit the ground running. Analyzing if I did that or not, I guess you would start with the record. Definitely there was an immediate improvement the first year, taking a team that had finished 5-26 overall and 0-18 in the league to 17-17 and 9-9, respectively. That was accomplished using the players and assets left from the previous year, save one transfer player I brought in. However, I think you need to look at the entire body of work to make an assessment. I'd throw out the overall record, since most of our non-conference games were on the road and were against a higher level of competition. Using the league record is probably most appropriate. Over my years at BC, our league record was 110-125, or said another way, our average league record on a yearly basis was 9-10. That is certainly nothing to write home about. We were simply an average team record-wise during my time as head coach. So analyzing the benefit to BC from a record standpoint, I'd say they could have probably done better hiring an experienced coach.

Moving beyond the record, the next question is, "Did I rebuild the infrastructure?" Reviewing **Exhibit 13**, I believe the answer is a resounding "Yes." There simply was no comparison of what type of assets existed in 2010 versus 1998. In addition to all the physical improvements and significant changes in how we could recruit, how much money could be awarded in scholarships, the size of the squad, etc., I also left $30,000 in the bank for the next coach to use at his discretion the following season. So from this perspective, I doubt they could have done any better hiring someone else.

Did I re-establish a winning mind-set? Again, I believe the answer is yes. We had a terrific season going in late January 2010, before injuries and illness wiped out our entire front line. The kids came to win every day at practice and on game day. There no longer was the doubt about winning that had existed for years. They were good and believed in themselves and each other. Reaching No. 14 in the country in only our second year of NAIA D1 simply confirmed this mind-set. The stimulus for this change was the additional resources available my last two years, allowing me to recruit a higher caliber of player. The only question to be asked here is, "Would another coach been able to do this sooner than I did?" That, unfortunately, is an unknown.

Finally, did I stabilize the program? I believe I did. For 12 years we followed a philosophy both on and off of the court that, if followed, would lead to success.

Interestingly, the third year after my departure, the team qualified for the national tournament. It was the first time in 45 years for BC's men's basketball team. It is a testament to the fine job that was done not only coaching, but also recruiting, by the second coach hired after I left. (The initial replacement quit after one year.) But it is also a testament, I believe, to the foundation that was built over the previous 12 to 13 years prior to his arrival. He benefited from not only the changes made during my tenure, but also those made in the year or two after I left. (I know that the President made some additional changes to benefit the basketball program after I left, for his decision to fire me was not a popular one among the college staff, the Abbey, the Convent, the local fans, or the alumni. An example of an additional change was with my successor, the college's Advancement organization, which is responsible for fund raising for the college, now assists the basketball program in raising funds each year.)

So overall, I believe the program was stabilized and was not in need of any "shoring up" in any areas at the time of my departure.

Personal Perspective

Looking at the 1998 decision from a personal perspective, I really have mixed feelings. The stress of trying to re-establish the winning mind-set, the frustration of getting so little help from the administration, the frustration of losing so much more than I had ever experienced as a player or player/coach, and the stress of the 2-hour roundtrip drive to Atchison for 12 years took its toll on my health. I began experiencing atrial fibrillation  (afib, or heart arrhythmia) in 2007 and eventually had a pacemaker implanted in 2008 and a heart ablation surgery in 2009. (I fully recovered from the afib after the ablation and am happy to say I still play full court basketball at age 71 against the 20- and 30-year olds at the community center.) Health issues are not an anomaly when it comes to college basketball coaches. (Skip Prosser at Wake Forest, Rick Majerus at Utah and St. Louis U., Lute Olson at Arizona...) I believe it is the stress of the job that contributes to these health issues, and I was not excluded from being affected.

Much of the stress I put on myself. I hate to lose, and all the losing really got to me. This is not to say I wouldn't have suffered the same fate had I stayed at Bell. With not knowing if you were going to have a job or not due to corporate buyouts and downsizing, that can put a lot of stress on you too. Plus, I personally believe part of the reason I got afib was due to my doctor prescribing statins for me to reduce my LDL (bad cholesterol). I started taking the medicine about two years before I had an emergency episode, and from day 1 felt strange. I ended up with having a pacemaker implanted in 2008. That probably would have occurred anyway had I still been at Bell.

Therefore, I'd probably say it is a wash when it comes to saying I would have been better off physically with either position.

Beyond the physical, mentally and spiritually I think I did fine. I was challenged mentally by having to learn and keep up with the current basketball philosophies and strategies, plus I still taught one of the capstone courses in the Executive MBA program at BC. The latter really challenges you mentally, for teaching strategic management to executives is not like teaching an introductory business course to undergrads. In the EMBA class, you better know your stuff and be current with your thinking or else you will be crucified. Had I stayed at Bell, the mental challenge would have come from staying current in your area of expertise. This isn't the same kind of challenge as one where you are learning something new or teaching a higher-level MBA class. So, from a mental perspective, I think I was better off in the coaching position.

Spiritually, my coaching/teaching schedule allowed me to go to daily Mass, which is a great way to start your day. I was also able to share my faith with young men who may not have been exposed to spirituality without having been part of the BC basketball program. In St. Louis, my wife and I drove downtown for work early enough to go to daily Mass at a downtown church, so that part is a wash for me. But sharing your faith/spirituality with your co-workers was limited in the business setting, so taking the BC coaching job was one up on staying in the Bell job as far as spirituality is concerned.

Summary

Taking each item above and choosing between staying at Bell and taking the coaching position at BC, here is what I have determined:

1. **Job Perspective** – Hands down the BC coaching position. It was a dream, and had I turned it down, I would have always wondered how I would have done compared to whoever they would have hired. There were many trials and disappointments, but being a part of the hundreds of young lives and helping shape them was not only satisfying, but it was an honor.

2. **Basketball Program Perspective** – Except for the "Dream" part of this, this one is a wash in my mind. I really made a difference building the infra-structure, creating a winning mind-set, and stabilizing the program. Maybe BC President Dan Carey had the foresight to hire me to be the "middle-man." I was to stop the bleeding, revive the patient, and renew the patient's strength so that the next physician could return the patient to full health. Maybe that was my role in the big picture. In my mind, though, an average yearly record in the league of 9-10 is not good enough. It offsets the value I added in the other areas and begs the question as to someone else being better suited to accomplish all of these things, not just the "middleman" parts.

3. **Personal Perspective** – Staying at Bell probably was a better decision. From a financial perspective, this is a no-brainer. But I say staying at Bell would have been better from the standpoint of my health, not money. The frustration of not being able to accomplish my goal was constantly on my mind, and no matter how hard I tried, I was never able to get us over the hump at BC. It affected me negatively, so staying at Bell would probably have been wiser. However, had I stayed at Bell I would have forever wondered if I would have been a successful turn-around coach at my alma mater. That in itself would have driven me nuts.

Conclusion

Now do you see why the question, "Knowing what you know today, if you could go back to 1998 would you make the same decision you did then and leave corporate America to coach college basketball at Benedictine College" is so hard to answer? From three perspectives I have one for BC, one a wash, and one for Bell. It's really a toss-up.

However, in 2018-19 the Ravens went 31-4, had a 29-game winning streak (breaking the 23 game streaks of our '64-'65 and '66-'67 teams), and ended the season ranked No. 1 in NAIA D1. Their coach, Ryan Moody, was National NAIA D1

Coach of the Year, and they advanced to the second round of the national tournament before losing a double overtime game. Coach Moody has taken BC to the national tournament 4 times in his eight years. The success I had strived for has been realized by Coach Moody. He got it done!

So looking back 10 years after I left the program, I can be a little more objective and a lot less emotional in analyzing just where I fit in in the grand scheme of things. I truly believe I was the "middle innings guy" or the "set up man," using baseball lingo. Just like I preached to my teams, each person has a role to play in order for the team to achieve success. My role was to be the "set-up man." What I did was definitely needed, and it was up to the next guy in line to close the deal and leverage those improvements into more success on the court. Coach Moody did that, and did it well.

I've referenced spirituality and the Bible numerous times in this book, and I think the conclusion I've reached concerning my role can also be shown to have happened many times in scripture. Just think of all the "set-up" men – Moses for Joshua, David for Solomon, John the Baptist for Jesus...the list goes on. Now I'm not trying to compare myself spiritually to any of these great people, but my role was similar, I believe. Moses spent 40 years in the desert preparing the Israelites for the Promised Land, but he did not get to lead them into it – Joshua did. David spent a lifetime creating a unified and wealthy nation, but did not get to build the magnificent Jewish Temple – Solomon did. And John the Baptist literally gave his life in preparing the Jews for Jesus and His message, but was murdered by Herod before seeing any of Jesus' fruit. They were all "set-up" guys. Their role was critical to good things happening in the immediate future. If it is accurate saying that what I did building the foundation that Coach Moody inherited when he took over a year after I left assisted him in achieving the Ravens' subsequent success, then "YES", I would make the same decision today I did back in 1998! After all, I got to live my Dream of being a college basketball coach. But more importantly, my initial goal has been achieved - the Ravens are back! You see, this isn't about me and never was – it is and always has been about **Raven Basketball**.

So, You Want to Be a Coach ... Lesson #12:
You only have one life to fulfill your dream – don't waste it.

Chapter 13: What Is It About Men and the "Dream of Coaching"?

"Success isn't just about what you accomplish in your life: it's about what you inspire others to do." (LearningStationMusic.com)

At the beginning of the book I had stated that there were so many people, regardless of their current position, who would say if they could do anything they wanted, what would it be - it would be a coach. Why is that?

My experience with this phenomenon has been mainly with men (thereby the name of this chapter), but I'm sure in today's environment this will also be true for many women. Again, from my experience, many men uniquely identify with a sport, and as they play it or watch it over a period of time, they feel like they become "experts" at knowing what to do and when to do it. The sports opinion shows on the radio and TV are extremely popular because of this very fact. "Monday morning quarterbacking" has become a profession for some. Second guessing others who are in coaching positions is almost a national pastime for a large portion of America's sports-crazed society. But why? Admit it, if you will – how many times have you been sitting on the couch watching a game and screamed at the TV, "Why did you do that"? I still do it, and I've been on the other side of the equation where the players don't always do what they have been taught or instructed to do from the bench. Still, it is the coach who is held accountable and chastised for decisions that you presume he/she made. Most of us think we could have done a better job and would love to be given the opportunity to do so.

On the surface, thinking you could do a better job than those who are paid to do it (coaching) may appear to be the main reason men (and some women) think they want to be a coach. But I believe there is more to it than that. Actually, I think the desire to coach is part of most people's DNA. I believe it is the desire to be a leader; I believe it is the desire to be successful; I believe it is the desire to make decisions and not be "harnessed" in any way; I believe it is the desire for timely and measurable feedback; but most of all I believe it is an <u>innate desire to help others excel</u>.

I have met many people in my 70+ years on God's great planet who have wanted to be a leader, successful, free to make decisions, and wanting to know honestly how they did. But I don't think that goes far enough in explaining why men/women want to coach. I believe there is a spiritual aspect to it also. It is my opinion that God implanted in each of us His desire that He has to make us as good as we can be. I believe it manifests itself when we reach out and help others. The "good feeling" that we have when we do this is God's way of showing us that he is smiling. I think coaching is an extension of this "spark", if you will, that is in each of us. When you coach, you share your knowledge and expertise with someone who does not have that knowledge or expertise. You assist in making them better. Your reward is simply the satisfaction to see that person improve or excel. That is God-like.

Coaching teams is just an extension of coaching individuals. The biggest difference between individual coaching and team coaching is that now you have added a level of what I'll call "virtues" to the equation. In a team environment, you not only help them as individuals, you also teach them how to sacrifice self for the betterment of the team. You teach them that each individual has a role to play and show them that if they play their role, the team output total will exceed the sum of its parts. In business they call it *synergy*. In team sports they call it *chemistry*.

One of the ways I tried to teach this lesson to my teams was by arranging for an "overnight" stay at a local Atchison team training facility. This was an outdoors training course located south of town that incorporated various stations located on the wooded grounds that specifically taught trust and teamwork to groups. The leader was a professionally trained person who would take the group through the various stations and force them into physical situations where they had to trust their teammates in order to safely accomplish a task or work together with one or more teammates, each with a specific role, to achieve a desired outcome. The course had zip lines, towers in trees, huge logs that you had to move, etc. that were used as props for each lesson. (The camp was extremely careful to protect the safety of the individuals, but it was still a little scary when you had to trust a teammate to be there when you fell backwards and they had to catch you.) There were about 8 stations in total, as I recall, each one targeting some form of trust or teamwork concept. All 22-24 players and I would drive out to the camp on a

Friday afternoon after classes on a nice September day and bring our overnight bags in preparation for the Friday night/Saturday morning training. The leader would take all of us through the physical training course on Friday afternoon/evening, and then we would use their barbeque pits to make hamburgers and brats for supper. After supper we would all meet in the large cabin on the grounds (it slept up to 25 people), and, as a group, would discuss the lessons learned that day. I would facilitate a discussion on how those lessons related to a basketball team and how that same trust and teamwork was necessary to be successful. I also would use some training tools and exercises I had learned at Bell to teach them how important "purpose" was and how all had to buy-in to that purpose for the team to be successful.

After the evening session was completed, I would break out the marshmallows and chocolate bars and make a campfire for anyone who wanted to make some s'mores. (Sounds hokey, but it was actually kinda fun – and who doesn't like s'mores?) In addition, the cabin had many board games and playing cards for the guests to use, which the players took full advantage of into the wee hours of the next day. The following morning the traditional breakfast was served – bacon and eggs with toast – all prepared by the seniors on the team. (I used this as a practical example of servant leadership.) At the culmination of breakfast and after cleaning up everything, everyone was free to go and enjoy the rest of their weekend.

This pre-season exercise gave us a head start on creating the chemistry we wanted to embrace in order for us to maximize our talents and abilities. Using non-sports setting enabled us to be able to emphasize the synergy/chemistry and role-playing concepts in a unique way, allowing the players to make a real-life analogy to what can be accomplished on the basketball court.

We have all seen this (synergy/chemistry drives unexpected success) work in experiences we have had both in sports and in other endeavors, but it seems like it is more prevalent in sports - or at least easier to cite examples. Here are a few examples that come to mind for me:

- Loyola's 1963 NCAA win over two-time defending champ Cincinnati
- The 1969 NY Jets beating the Baltimore Colts in Super Bowl III
- The 1980 "Miracle on Ice" USA hockey team winning the Olympics

- Jim Valvano's 1983 North Carolina State team beating Houston in the NCAA title
- The 2015 KC Royals beating the Mets in the World Series

The list could go on and on. The point is, there are times when a coach can put the pieces together and motivate players to do more collectively than they could do individually, and the satisfaction that brings to a coach is almost spiritual. It is an extension of the feeling I described above when you teach someone something that allows that person to be successful. Now it's even a richer experience, because it has been raised to the next level where you are affecting more than just one person. Men, especially sports-oriented men, witness these things and want to be a part of it. For that reason, I think men in general hold this notion of being a coach out as being a "dream job." My guess is that due to Title IX women now experience this phenomenon also.

So, You Want to be a Coach...Conclusion

"Bloom where you are planted." (St. Francis de Sales (1567 – 1622), Bishop of Geneva)

So where does this leave us as far as "Dream Jobs" go? My observation over my many years of being in business, athletics, and academia, is that you can experience these same things (leading individuals and groups to unexpected growth and success) regardless of the career path you follow. Think of the

"mentors" you have had in your life. They were not all sports coaches – but they were all coaches. Think of those younger folks in your life who you helped succeed – you were coaching them. Remember how happy you were for those who succeeded in part by your influence on them? That happiness was the "spark" I referred to earlier – that was part of God in you. We all have it, and we can all experience it right where we are. We don't have to be a sports "coach" for that light to shine.

I was blessed to be able to experience that light while performing my dream job (college head basketball coach), but unknowingly I had already experienced that light in business and in volunteer work. I got that thrill as the Assistant Treasurer at SW Bell when one of my subordinates would make a great presentation at a national conference on a new method they had developed for managing cash; or when my work group was recognized for making the most progress on a company-wide index for customer service. That thrill or light was the same at Bell as it was when our underdog team at BC beat the two-time defending national champs in a holiday classic. The dream actually was available at Bell as much as it was at BC. I just did not realize it.

Think about your current situation...if you have not experienced it already, isn't the opportunity at hand for you to bloom where you are planted? Take that step to "coach" someone, and your light will shine too. The ball is in your court.

So, You Want to Be a Coach … Lesson #13:
You don't have to have the title "Coach" to coach.

Exhibits

Big task ahead for Brickner

VIEWPOINT

Paul Suellentrop
Sports Editor

Welcome back to Benedictine, Joe. I'm sure your reception was warm, enthusiastic and filled with optimism. You're probably a surprise choice to many people, considering you don't have any formal coaching experience. I — as someone who has played basketball against you and talked basketball with you — have little doubt there's enough toughness, brains and desire there to coach and coach well.

Will that be enough to revive a program that — with a few exceptions — has been struggling since 1973? That's my big question. I know you want to win. My fear is you and your kind is in the minority on that campus. Oh, there's probably a lot of people who love the idea of winning basketball. Apparently there are few who actually can or will do something about it.

Benedictine's track record of 18 losing seasons in the last 28 years tells me there's more

wrong there than coaching. It's a long story of turbulent times with the merger of the men's and women's schools, financial difficulty and millions of other changes since the glory days of Raven basketball.

For whatever reason, winning basketball games never seemed a big priority in recent years. I think it's a pretty safe bet that nobody outside of the athletic department ever came to Mike

Sickafoose, your predecessor, and asked him what he needed to win. I don't think anybody ever really gave him a strong impression winning was important. If winning has been a priority over the past 25 years, that's a real bad sign.

You know, I'm not even sure winning should be important at Benedictine. If there's an extra $5,000 somewhere, maybe it should go to computers, new chalkboards or faculty raises. If Benedictine needs 12 kids to meet enrollment projections then why shouldn't the basketball team divide up its scholarship money and resources and start a junior varsity team?

Let the big schools spend outrageous amounts of money on sports. Benedictine should be a leader in sanity and putting academics first.

Joe, your son, Scott, played at Benedictine just a few years ago.

Please see **Big task/Page C6**

Big task ahead for new Benedictine head coach

Continued from Page C1

So you should have a pretty good idea about the long van rides, the fast food and the long hours. I hope you're as familiar with the inner workings of budgets, scholarships etc.

Let me give you an example: Benedictine men's and women's basketball teams had almost identical budgets this past year, as they should. Benedictine has a men's junior varsity team. The women don't. Same amount of money for both, but the men's money is spread out over more players and more games.

Is that the best way to build a winner? Probably not. It is, however, the best way to keep enrollment up.

That's the kind of thing that concerns me. Did Benedictine hire you to win games or act as an emergency admissions counselor? I hope this was spelled out during the interview.

Now with the right combination of hard work and good for-

tune, I think you can win at Benedictine. Del Morley and Sickafoose both won games — when they had good players. It's not going to be easy.

Your best bet is to raise money like crazy. William Jewell coach Larry Holley said his team raises around $30,000 each season to pay for a nice trip and other extras. I'm not sure Benedictine can raise that much, but every dollar will help. You're probably going to have to do it on your own.

Your first move should be to sit down with football coach Larry Wilcox and women's basketball coach Steve Huber. They're both excellent coaches who work tirelessly. Listen to every bit of advice Wilcox has for you.

Welcome back, Joe. It's a great school, and I think you're a great choice as head coach. I know you love Benedictine. I hope you're still in love and still coaching five years from now.

Exhibit 2: Daily Practice Schedule

Daily Practice Schedule

Date: 9/16/09		Day: Wednesday	Gym: Old 4:00 p.m.		Practice # 2
Time	Min.	Drill		Leader	Comments
4.00	0.03	Debusschere Drill		JB	Baseball pass to roll, dribble out, reverse pivot, 2-hand overhead pass to roll, shot fake & jumper
4.03	0.05	Seal Drill		JP	2 Groups
4.08	0.05	Closeout Drill		JP	Explain and Apply - Both Ends 2 groups each side
4.13	0.10	Push Drill		JP	Explain and Apply
4.23	0.08	Pentagonal Position		JP	Start with Closeout/Attack add Push
4.31	0.05	V-cut with shot		JB	Both ends, same side (1 passer, 1 cutter)
4.36	0.05	V-cut with pass to post then back pick		JB	Both ends, same side (1 passer, 1 cutter, 1 post - 2 balls)
4.41	0.02	Review setting pick & cutting principles		JB	Demonstrate - beat man to picker's shoulder/lower than picker's shoulder
4.43	0.07	3 on 0 Flex drill - 2 balls		JB	4 players, flex & down cutters are shooters
4.50	0.03	3 on 0 Flex drill - 2 balls (Add back cut to flex)		JB	Go under flex pick instead of over
4.53	0.05	Deny Position		JP	Demonstrate and apply in 2 on 1 scenario
4.58	0.07	Pentagonal Position		JP	Rollout to Deny to Attack
5.05	0.08	Dummy Flex (5 on 0) - 3 groups		3 Coaches	Sub in two extras.
5.13	0.07	Rebounding Outlet Drill		JB	Turn in air, outlet to wing, pass to middle, turn back at half-court for 2 on 1 (Rebounder must go to 3 point line)
5.20	0.04	Defensive Make-up drill		JP	
5.24	0.04	Offensive Make-up drill		JB	Both ends. Sub in two extras.
5.28	0.02	Communication Drill		JB	
5.30		Jog & Stretch		Captains	

Groups:	1	Bonham	1	Johnson
	2	Harry	2	Williams, R.
	3	Bolling	3	Hamilton
	1	Miller	2	Demps
	3	Daniels	3	Seymore
	2	Anderson	2	Winn
	2	Williams, K.	1	Davis
	3	Corless		McNeil
	1	McFaul	X	Hund

163

THE 3F MODEL FOR SUCCESS

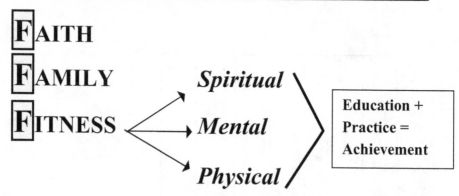

FAITH

FAMILY

FITNESS

Spiritual

Mental

Physical

Education +
Practice =
Achievement

JB's MANAGEMENT CREED

I believe...

- Each person wants to do their best.
- People will perform at peak levels if they are doing what they really want to do in life.
- People like being told (often & sincerely) that they do good work and are appreciated.
- Partnerships win.
- The "S" in success stands for "Sacrifice".
- Only dumb luck can beat working hard and working "smart".
- Proper planning and organizing build the foundation for attainment.
- The ability to communicate and the commitment to do so are vital to efficiency and effectiveness.
- Everyone must be a leader. Everyone must be a follower. Wisdom is knowing when to play which role.
- Leaders remove roadblocks and keep their group focused.
- Lessons learned from small failures pay big dividends.
- What goes around, comes around.
- In your retirement years, what will really count is the number of friendships you have cultivated, not the number of promotions you received.

Exhibit 3A: 3F Model Explanation

THE 3F MODEL FOR SUCCESS

This model describes how success can be achieved by focusing on three key factors: Faith, Family, and Fitness, specifically in that order.

Faith means putting God first in all that you do. If a person is capable of putting God first, everything else will take care of itself. But putting God first is a very difficult endeavor for most human beings. Putting God first does not only entail following the Ten Commandments and praising Him on a regular basis, but most importantly it means finding God's presence in every person we come in contact with each day.

Family means blood relation but can also extend beyond that to non-related friends and loved ones. In most cases it will mean tending to the needs of your parents, siblings, and children. These are the people that are going to be there for you when you need help - that is what family is all about, i.e., taking care of one another. Family should come right behind Faith.

Fitness means healthy. It is split into three components; *spiritual fitness, mental fitness, and physical fitness*. Each of these components require two key elements in order to achieve fitness: education and practice. In other words, without learning about how to be fit and then practicing what you have learned, you will never achieve fitness. (**Education + Practice = Achievement**) This formula must be followed in all three components (spiritually, mentally, and physically) in order to reach ultimate happiness and success. Failure to reach fitness in any one component will significantly lessen your success and happiness.

Mission & Goals

The mission of the Benedictine College Men's Basketball Program is to win a third NAIA National Championship, while developing young men into leaders who will make this world a better place in which to live.

- Our goals are simple: to win games on the court, and to change hearts off of the court.
  - o Integrity, aspiration, resilience, determination, and a Christian love for others create the foundation for achieving these goals.

As a program, we will make **the maximum effort** to achieve our mission.

Exhibit 5: In Pursuit of Excellence Form

Name: _____

Academic Goals: (Team Goal is Team GPA of 3.0 or better)

Overall GPA _____

Course	Professor	Credit Hours	Target Grade	Points
Total				

Plans to Achieve Goals:

1. _____
2. _____
3. _____
4. _____
5. _____

Exhibit 5: In Pursuit of Excellence Form (cont.)

Athletic Goals: (Team Goal is to Qualify for NAIA National Tournament)

Team Achievements:

A. _____

B. _____

C. _____

Individual Goals:

A. _____

B. _____

C. _____

Plans to Achieve Team & Individual Goals:

1. _____

2. _____

3. _____

4. _____

5. _____

Exhibit 5: In Pursuit of Excellence Form (cont.)

Spiritual Goals: (Team Goal is to grow closer to our Creator)

Service Goals:

   A. _____
   B. _____
   C. _____

"Quiet Time" Goals:

   A. _____
   B. _____
   C. _____

Plans to Achieve Team & Individual Goals:

   1. _____
   2. _____
   3. _____
   4. _____
   5. _____

Social Goals: (Team Goal is to experience the Joy of college life)

Campus Club Member:

_____

Meeting Attendance:

Sept	Oct	Nov	Dec/Jan	Feb	Mar	Apr

Attend a campus sporting/social event once/week:

Sept	Oct	Nov	Dec/Jan	Feb	Mar	Apr

Sit at table at lunch/dinner with at least two non-basketball players:

Sept	Oct	Nov	Dec/Jan	Feb	Mar	Apr

Exhibit 5: In Pursuit of Excellence Form (cont.)

Other Plans to Achieve Social Goals:

1. _____
2. _____
3. _____

What motivates me to succeed?

_____

_____

Exhibit 6: Time Management Handout

Time Management

Success Challenge: Balancing school, basketball, work, and family/social priorities - and excelling at all of them

Success Strategy: Clearly defining school and social responsibilities

1. Seize the day
Start each day (or you **should** do this the night before) with one "To-do" list, separating your personal tasks and school tasks. Keep the list in your notebook or planner and as you add To-do's throughout the day, continually evaluate your priorities, especially if your time is limited and you're working around your basketball schedule.

2. Break it up
Divide your To-do list into two categories: "Things to-do" and "Calls to Make". A long list is less overwhelming when it is divided into manageable parts. Make all of your calls at one time, adding action items to your To-do list.

3. Follow the rule, "Do it or delete it."
Before you automatically transfer a task from one daily list to another, determine why you haven't started it or if it even needs to be done. You may find that the task isn't important after all. Also, **reprioritize your list every night** for the next day.

4. Establish time for school, time for basketball - and quality social time
Follow the same schedule as much as possible. Inform friends/roommates of your class/study/practice/work hours. Awaken at the same time each day, and try to go to bed at the same time each weekday.

5. Communicate your schedule
Post a monthly calendar in a central location like the refrigerator. Schedule business (school, basketball, and work) and social commitments using different colored pens. Roommates, etc. can refer to this when determining if you are available or not, especially if your class/practice schedule requires irregular times.

6. Organize your desk space in your room, and keep it uncluttered. File items in folders as they are used, so that you don't spend time looking for that "lost" paper/report.

7. Schedule one-hour blocks
Large tasks won't seem so overwhelming when broken into hour-long chunks of time. To help you concentrate, allow voice mail to pick up the phone. This is also a good method to use when you have a task that you do not want to do – break it up into littler pieces, and do a little bit each day.

8. Mind the store
Dedicate a small amount of time -- one hour or so -- each day for placing calls, writing letters, purging files and paying bills to keep small but necessary tasks from piling up.

Study Techniques

1. Read text
   A. Highlight important concepts
   B. Do practice problems
2. Attend class
   A. Take notes (Demonstration)
3. Review notes same day as notes were taken, filling in the blanks, etc.
   A. Summarize in left margin
4. Do homework assignments
5. Study for Exams
   A. Review text, especially highlighted areas
   B. Review notes, and highlight most important concepts

Exhibit 7: Successful Study Techniques Handout

SUCCESSFUL STUDY TECHNIQUES

1. Review notes ASAP after class. Highlight points stressed by the professor during the lecture.

2. Try to study the same subject at the same time each day.

3. Try to study in the same place each day. Use that place for studying, ONLY!!

4. Preview material. If assigned a chapter in a textbook, read:
   a. title and introduction
   b. headings, subheadings, topic sentences
   c. boldfaced/italicized words
   d. chapter summary and any review questions
   THEN, read the chapter . . .

5. As you read, examine every graph, chart, illustration carefully.

6. Note in the textbook's margins any points you don't understand or any questions you need answered by your professor.

7. Draw a diagram or map of the material using any shape you want to organize your material and thoughts.

8. Make your own flashcards for terms. Words on one side, definitions on the back. Go through the cards REPEATEDLY until you can define each word correctly.

9. Invent Acrostics; i.e., Peter Ate Ink = Pacific, Atlantic, and Indian Oceans in order of size. . . These are sentences in which the first letter of each work is the same as the first letter of each word you need to remember.

10. To memorize a quotation or a series of numbers, break it up into smaller segments. Memorize the first part, then the second, then put the two together. OR, memorize from the bottom up – especially good for poetry.

Exhibit 8: Test-Taking Tips

TEST-TAKING TIPS

FOR SHORT-ANSWER EXAMS:

1. Estimate how much time you have to answer each question. If some questions are worth more points than others, plan to spend more time answering them.
2. Do the easiest questions first.
3. Write what you do know – even if you don't know the complete answer. (The very *act* of writing may spark your memory.)
4. *Never leave early!!* Review your answers, make corrections, add more information . . .

FOR ESSAY EXAMS:

1. Read all of the questions first. <u>Underline</u> key words, such as "discuss", "explain", and "compare". THEN, jot down your initial thoughts.
2. Start with the easiest questions. Draft your answer, leaving space between lines and in margins. For rewrites/corrections.
3. Use short, simple sentences to make your points.
4. Answer more difficult questions last. *Use all of the allotted time.*

OBJECTIVE EXAMS – MULTIPLE CHOICE, MATCHING, ETC:

1. Solve questions in the order given. Circle ones you "skip" and return to them if time permits.
2. Read each choice carefully. Beware of words like: "often", "sometimes", and "always". Select the answer that is **most** correct. (Even wrong answers may be partially true.)
3. <u>**THINK AS YOU READ!!**</u> Eliminate the choices you know are wrong and then make an "educated" guess.
4. Finish the exam – then go back to any questions you skipped, use all of the time allowed.

Exhibit 9: Weightlifting Schedule

4 Day Weightlifting Workout

Monday	Tuesday	Wed	Thursday	Friday
Chest, Back, & Shoulders 3 Sets (80% @ 8 reps)	**Legs & Arms** 3 Sets (80% @ 8 reps)	OFF	**Chest, Back, & Shoulders** 3 Sets (60% @ 12 reps)	**Legs & Arms** 3 Sets (60% @ 12 reps)
Bench Press	Squats or Leg Press		Bench Press	Squats or Leg Press
Dumb Bell Inclines	Leg Extensions		Dumb Bell Inclines	Leg Extensions
Pushups	Leg Curls		Pushups	Leg Curls
Pec Dec	Hip Flexors		Pec Dec	Hip Flexors
Pull Ups	Bicep Curl		Pull Ups	Bicep Curl
Low Cable Rows	Tricep Extension		Low Cable Rows	Tricep Extension
High Pulls	Straight Leg Dead Lift		High Pulls	Straight Leg Dead Lift
Shoulder Press			Shoulder Press	
Shoulder Shrugs			Shoulder Shrugs	

You should do Plyometrics after you lift, but it should only last about 5 minutes. Do these twice per week after you've lifted for your legs.

Drop Box (3 sets of 5)
Bench Jump (5 sets of 5)

General Notes:

Force X Mass = Acceleration (F*M=A)
Stabilization is Critical. Stabilize your Core, Joints, and Back when lifting.
Constant Motion is Critical. Do not stop when you extend or contract while performing an exercise.
Do not lift too fast. You do not want momentum to help you lift a weight.
Do not lift for longer than 1 hour.
Recovery requires 48 hours. (Be sure to get 8 hours sleep per night.)
Take **Vitamin Supplements.** Eat fruits and vegetables. Drink lots of **water.**

For more information, go to **www.popeyescardio.com.**

175

Exhibit 10: Nutrition Example

Nutrition 101

Determining Your Daily Energy Needs

Desired Weight * Daily Rate * Activity Factor

0.64 = Low

= Calories (KCAL)   0.68 = Moderate

0.73 = High

Example:

180 lbs * 24 hrs. * 0.64 = 2765 KCAL

Summary

180 lb. man with Low Activity and Maintaining Muscle Mass

Carbs = 415
Protein = 83
Fat = 77

What Benedictine Needs To Win At NAIA D1 Level

I. Bottom Line:

I have no personal or political agenda. I love Benedictine College, and have been a player, an alumnus, a parent of a player, and a coach at BC. I feel I have a unique and somewhat complete viewpoint of Raven basketball over the last 41 years.

The bottom line is: if you fund it, we will win.

- We need 9 full scholarships for 13-14 players. (However, I have already committed money to 16 players, 12-13 of which are not NAIA D1 material). Therefore, for at least 2-3 years, I need extra money to honor my commitments to the original players (the right thing to do) and still be able to recruit NAIA D1 level players.
    - You can't get good players if they have to pay to play. Even though we are going NAIA D1, the Benedictine tuition discount formula still applies. Scholarships have to average 60% of tuition. Next year, this gives me about $11,300 per player, but Benedictine costs $25,200 per year. So, on average, each freshman has to pay $14,000 a year for the "privilege" of playing basketball at Benedictine, and seniors living in the apartments would have to pay $15,400. This tremendously limits the level of player that is recruitable.
        - To put this in perspective, for every freshman who receives a full scholarship, I have to recruit 2 players who only receive $4320 in total scholarship assistance. (For a senior, I'd have to get two players at $3635 each in total scholarships.)

- We need at least $40,000 per year operating budget (less ticket sales revenue), not including salaries for coaches. (I currently receive $21,296 per year for my operating budget). This $40,000 would be for:

- o Officials & other home game expenses
- o Equipment & Apparel (shoes, practice & game uniforms, travel apparel, balls, etc.)
- o Travel expenses for each road game (gas, food)
  - ▪ Big bus rental for safety when traveling away for long distance games. (Culver, Lindenwood, Evangel, Central Methodist)
  - ▪ Bus driver for games closer to campus
- o Administrative costs (postage, phones, Media Guide printing, etc.)
- o Meal expenses during holidays when campus is closed
- o Cost of trip at Thanksgiving or Christmas time so that we can play in front of the families and friends of out-of-state recruits.
- o Recruiting expenses (travel costs for official visits as well as reimbursement for coaches traveling to watch/visit potential recruits.)
  - ▪ I need travel money to get 5 to 10 recruits to visit from out of state. (At approximately $300 per flight, this will cost between $1500 and $3,000 to fly recruits to Atchison). This can be done according to NAIA rules as long as Benedictine's policy for reimbursement is the same for any specially gifted student, not just athletes. At this time, recruits are reimbursed up to $75 for public transportation. The $75 has been the limit for at least the past 10 years, I believe.
    - • Since we recruit from a national scope, this would really enhance our ability to sign top talent. I have lost a number of very good prospects because they would have to pay for transportation to make a visit to BC. They do not have to pay for transportation to visit an NCAA D2 school, and that is our major competition for this level of talent.

    - • It would also be beneficial to be able to reimburse selected recruits for driving expenses. With the price of gas escalating, we may not be able to get a recruit from as near as St. Louis to drive in without

helping out with the travel expense.
(NCAA rules allow this.)

- We need for players' classes to be available outside of practice times.

- We need consistent times in the Nolan Gymnasium to practice, preferably at 3 p.m. in the afternoon, when all players can make all practices.

- We need a volunteer network to help recruit.

- We need the basketball suite to be the basketball suite and be identified as such. The new offices will significantly increase the credibility of our program from a recruit's perspective.

- We need adequate storage space in Nolan.
  o Storage space in Nolan is extremely limited. We have no place to store equipment and apparel over and above the space available in our locker rooms, which is full. We need storage areas in addition to the west storage room. Richard Konzem's plan was to use Mary Lile's office for basketball equipment storage (Mary was moving into Joe Brickner's old office), and to also use the intramural room behind the small office at the east end of the gym for basketball filing & equipment storage.

- We need an experienced Assistant Coach, who can make a living being an Assistant Coach. The current coach makes $21,000 per year and must find "odd jobs" throughout the year just to make ends meet.

- We need a band, cheerleaders, and students to support the team to create an atmosphere that will give us the home court advantage we used to have in the old gym.
  o I need a campus-wide coordinated schedule so that no other events are scheduled during the basketball games. This will help get students and fans in the stands.

II. Opinions:

Some may believe that the men's program should copy the women's program or the football program in order to achieve success. I'm sure it's been discussed more than once over a cup of coffee. Listed below are items that discuss certain facts, including these two lines of thinking.

A. Discussion of men's versus women's basketball

These are two totally different animals, and really can't be compared to one another. The men play in the best conference in the country, (2 national championships in the last 7 years, always getting at least one team to the final four) with some of the best coaches in the country at the helm of extremely stable programs (Lamar – 26 years at MNU, Holley – 31 years at WJ, Jenkins – 27 years at Evangel, Sherman – 16 years at CMU, etc.). The women's programs in the league are not nearly as competitive at the national level, and their coaching staffs turn over quite often. (This in no way diminishes the accomplishments of Chad Folsom. I personally think he is a great coach and would do well on the men's side as well as on the women's side.) The range of talent between a low college level player and a high-level college player is significantly less than that of men. Women's egos are not nearly as large as men's egos, and a gal will go to a college because she feels she fits – a guy has to go to the highest level on a full ride or else he is a failure in his own eyes. These are just a few of the differences, and there are many more that simply won't allow a fair comparison to be made. Therefore, the needs of the women's program may be significantly different than the needs of the men's program in order to be successful and should be analyzed separately.

B. Discussion of football's strategy used for basketball

Football gets 160 - 170 recruits. (Most at them receive minimal scholarship assistance.) This allows football to offer larger scholarships to their best players if they choose to do so. (Side note: Football suffers even more than basketball from the artificial limitations dictated by their tuition discount formula). Below are the reasons why the football strategy will not work for basketball:

- Football is not limited by facilities as basketball is.
    - Football has a large practice field and soon will have a game field that could be used for practice also. (Basketball has 6 baskets in Nolan or 4 baskets in the old gym to use during practice. It's hard enough find facilities large enough for 20 players to practice in, much less 30. Also,

180

we only have 24 lockers in our locker room, which limits the number of players unless you separate them by using the visitors' locker room.

- Football has about 15 volunteers from the Atchison area to help coach such a large squad. However, it is easier to get volunteers for football due to the limited length of the season and the predictability of practice and game times.
    - Football practices at 3PM M-F. (Basketball bounces around between afternoon and evening practices due to the contention for practice time in the gym(s), i.e., Volleyball and Men's and Women's basketball)
    - Football games are at 1PM or 2PM every Saturday. (Basketball games are played from November through possibly mid-March, with games being played on any night during the week and in the afternoon on weekends. Such a schedule is difficult for volunteers.)
    - Weather is normally not a factor for football travel. (Weather is a huge travel factor for basketball, which can limit a volunteer's ability to attend practice or accompany the team to games.)

C. Location, Location, Location

MNU, William Jewell, and Evangel have been at the top of the HAAC for years. All three enjoy a distinct advantage from the standpoint of being located in a metropolitan area. Atchison, Kansas is a small rural community. Kansas City schools enjoy the luxury of the following:

- Assistants who volunteer to help them. MidAmerica has 5 assistants (3 unpaid) who can go to every game and every practice, and recruit and scout for them also. William Jewell has 6 assistants. (3 unpaid)

- MidAmerica and William Jewell (both in Kansas City) have consistently gone to the NAIA D2 tournament (MidAmerica – 10 straight years, William Jewell – 4 of the last 10, Evangel, in Springfield, MO, has gone 5 times in the last 10 years.) The only other school to go to the tournament during that time is Lindenwood, who has gone twice. Lindenwood is in St. Charles, right outside of St. Louis. No other teams in small, rural areas (Baker-Baldwin City; Graceland-Lamoni, Iowa; Missouri Valley-Marshall, MO; Central Methodist-Fayette, MO; Culver-Stockton – Canton, MO) have gone to the tournament in the last 10 years.

- Benedictine was a major contender in the NAIA until 1972, when St. Benedict's and Mount St. Scholastica merged. Shortly after that, the Benedictine administration forced the basketball program to recruit 24 athletes with its 10 scholarships, instead of 12-13 athletes with 10 scholarships as was the case when SBC was a small college power in the 60's. Not coincidently, starting in 1972, Benedictine's success declined. We've only had 8 winning seasons (more wins than losses) in 36 years since 1972. When the scholarships were not diluted, we had 9 consecutive winning seasons (1963-1972).
- In 1991, scholarships were diluted further when the Benedictine administration decided to go to the NAIA Division 2 level instead of staying NAIA Division 1 or following Washburn, Hays, etc. into NCAA D2. At this point, scholarships were reduced to 5, but the number of players required to be recruited remained at 20-24. At the same time, Benedictine joined the Heart of America Conference, and had to compete at a disadvantage due to the number of scholarships awarded by schools like William Jewell and MidAmerica.

III. Kansas City Resources versus Atchison Resources

A. Recruiting
Totally different opportunity for recruiting (Kansas City area versus Atchison), as addressed above.

B. Basketball camps
MidAmerica and William Jewell conduct basketball camps each summer. MidAmerica earns over $200,000 doing this, and William Jewell earns an unknown amount, but it is at least six figures. We have tried to hold basketball camps in Atchison in order to help our Assistant Coach earn more money. However, they are poorly attended due to the average income in Atchison and the lack of attendees due to the small population of the town. (18 campers two years ago and 14 campers last summer.) MidAmerica and William Jewell have a large attendance due to their location and the long history of hosting camps. Because of these camps:

- They take part of their proceeds and funnel it back into their operating budget. (I have been told by both head coaches that they spend $80K per year on their basketball programs, a large portion via the summer camp contributions.)
  - MidAmerica also funnels money from their camps back into scholarships for their current players.
- They "plant the recruiting seed" while the kids attending their camps are still in grade school.
- They employ their players to give them a summer job.
  - This also allows the players to play together every night during the summer, creating team chemistry on and off the court.
- WJ employs local referees.

C. Players living at home in KC

MidAmerica and William Jewell have an advantage in recruiting the Kansas City players because many continue to live at home while attending college. This allows these two teams to give a KC player a full tuition scholarship so they do not have to pay anything to attend school. This option is not available in Atchison. KC is too far away for KC kids to live at home, and there is seldom a player from Atchison who is good enough in basketball and in the classroom to attend BC. This causes each BC player, therefore, to pay about $7,000 for room and board per year that an MNU or WJ player does not have to pay. This is not only an advantage from a player's cost standpoint, but it also allows these two schools to offer more "full rides" than other schools who must include room and board in a player's scholarship.

- For example, if we set the costs of the schools at the exact same level (tuition = $18K, overall cost = $25K) and assume that 7 full scholarships are the limit, then the pool available is $175K. (7 times $25K) If a player lives at home, the school can give 9.7 full rides ($175K/$18K) as opposed to 7 for a school whose players live and eat on campus. This is expanded even further if a school doesn't count "exempt" players in their $175K limit.

D. Players stay in KC in the summer.

Because the players work at the KC camps and many live in KC, the team plays together all summer long. This enhances their success because they practice in advance of the season.

E. Facilities

MidAmerica has 3 full court facilities, so the men can practice at the same time as the women's team practices. William Jewell has 4 full court facilities and can do the same. At Benedictine, there is constant contention for Nolan Gymnasium due to multiple sports and other miscellaneous functions held in the gym by non-athletic organizations. During first semester we can use the Old Gym, but with volleyball still in season, one of the teams has to practice at night. During the second semester the old gym is not available, so once again, even though volleyball has ended, one of the teams has to practice at night.

F. Volunteers can go to KC games to recruit

With all of the volunteers for the KC schools, they always have someone to go to KC high school games to watch recruits. I cannot attend games, because I have practice many times at night. With 20 or more players on the roster, I also need the Assistant Coach to help me at practice. Although Jackson Wood helped at practices, he has a regular full-time teaching job and cannot always allow time to go to KC games. Plus, when I send John Peer or Jackson to KC games, I have to reimburse them for gas money, which can run $60.00 per trip. This eats into my limited basketball budget. (If I am able to go to a KC game, I normally don't turn in expenses because I live in KC.) However, MidAmerica and William Jewell, because of all of their assistants, can send many of their volunteers out to watch high school games throughout the area with limited expense.

IV. Why Going NAIA D1 is a good idea for Benedictine

- A minimum of 3 teams will go to the national tournament instead of two. Plus, with the significantly larger number of "at large" bids, our league could eventually get 4 or 5 league teams into the tournament like the Sooner Conference does today.
- The National Tournament is held in Kansas City.
  - Media coverage is very high in the KC area, whereas the Branson tournament gets minimal coverage.
  - It will excite the local KC Benedictine fans and be close for Atchison locals to attend the NAIA tournament. (It has the possibility of creating the level of excitement that was prevalent in the '60's.)

- Games are broadcast on national TV (semifinals & finals are on CSTV), again creating the opportunity for Conference Schools to become known nationally.
- It's a higher level of competition, so it allows us to recruit a better athlete.
  - Allows us to give a larger scholarship, enabling us to sign better athletes.
  - Better competition (many NCAA D1 transfers) will entice better players to enroll. (The top players don't want to play at NAIA Division Level 2, because it's viewed as the lowest level in college sports. Men basketball players have large egos, and many won't even give you the time of day if they know you are an NAIA D2 or NCAA D3 school.)
- Upgrades the level of competition for the fans, so the games will be more entertaining.
- Will allow us to compete with NCAA Division 2 schools in our non-conference portion of our schedule, thus raising the reputation and credibility of schools in our conference.
- It "helps" level the playing field among schools in our conference. The top teams in the HAAC were giving over 9 scholarships for approximately 13 players by using exempt players to legally exceed the six-scholarship limit. Now, even if they continue to go over the eventual 9 limit level due to exempts, it will not have as big an impact as before, since you can only play 5 at a time! Their benches may be deeper, but their starting five should be comparable to a school who stays within the 9-scholarship level.
  - I do want to stress that location is still a major negative factor for all schools located in small, rural towns

V. My accomplishments in NAIA D2 in spite of the above limitations:

- Since I came in 1998-99, Benedictine has now become competitive in NAIA Div. 2. Although we have not made it to the tournament, my record has been better than any BC coach since Tom Colwell in 1971-1976. We are now respected in the league and have been ranked nationally for the first time in nearly 40 years.
  - The year before I became coach, the team was 5-26 overall, and 0-18 in the HAAC. I only had time to recruit

185

1 player, but we still went 17-17 overall and 9-9 in the HAAC my first year. We beat 2nd place Evangel in Springfield in the playoffs and have been respected in the league ever since that time.

- We are known for playing the best (toughest) non-conference schedule in the league, which causes our overall record to suffer, but gets us physically ready to play in the best D2 league in the nation.

- We were No. 2 in the HAAC in 2006-2007 season. It was the first time since BC joined the league (1991) that Benedictine came in second.

- We finished 3rd in the league in 2003-2004. It was only the second time since BC joined the league (1991) that Benedictine came in third. (BC actually finished third that year with an 8-8 record.)
  - Both of these years ('06-'07 & '03-'04) we won 14 league games. This is the most league wins by any Benedictine team since BC joined the Conference.

- Although we came in 6th out of 11 this year, Benedictine's increased competitive level was exemplified by our beating the No. 1 team in the nation (MidAmerica), and losing to Bellevue (the National runners-up) by one possession on their home court, where they had won 37 games in a row. Even in the playoffs, after we had experienced a stretch of losses in the second half of the year, we nearly beat the hottest team in the league (Central Methodist) on their home court. Had the officiating been consistent both halves, we probably would have won the game by double digits.

- I'm the only Coach in the history of the school, other than Ralph Nolan, to win 20 games in a season (2006-2007).

- I recruited and coached the first all-American (Dan Van Dyke) at BC since Chic Downing in was named in 1972. (Van Dyke was a back-up center at Bishop Miege high school.)

- Although it appears that WJ and MNU get more KC area recruits than BC, note that 4 of our top 6 players in 2007-08 were KC kids. (Van Dyke, Huppe – Aquinas, Larson – Liberty, and John-

186

son – Mill Valley) Larson, from tradition rich Liberty high school, was the top KC area recruit in the entire HAAC. He was first team Class 5 All-state, league MVP, All-Metro, etc., and has personally told me that I am the reason he signed with BC.

- I continue to fund raise:
    - So that the players don't have to buy their own shoes and equipment, and to make up for the operating budget's shortfall each year.
    - In order to take trips, which enhances recruiting
    - To buy capital items to improve facilities. (Pit bleachers, Nautilus equipment in old gym, chairs for games, lighted scorer's tables for games, gym painting, new basketball suite, etc.)
    - To increase scholarships (Anonymous donor $100K over 4 years because we went NAIA D1)

- Our players stay 4 years (sometimes 4.5 or 5 years) and graduate. Very seldom do my players transfer to other schools. Even those who leave the team prematurely stay and graduate. (e.g., Andre Finner, Scott McEvoy)

- I try to bring a spirituality to the team by being the only team on campus with its own Chaplain, praying as a team before every practice and before and after every game, and talking about and teaching the young men to "do the right thing, even when no one is watching". I believe if I can plant the spirituality seed now and show these young men that it is okay for a man to pray and talk about his faith and his God, that somewhere down the line it's going to make a difference in their life.

VI. My Plan to Become Competitive at the NAIA D1 Level

A. Recruiting

- We must recruit either NCAA D1 or Junior College transfers to supplement our current roster. This is the only way to immediately impact the talent level we need to compete.

187

- We must target top talented high school juniors and seniors as prospective recruits, and only bring in players capable of excelling at the NAIA D1 level.

- We must continue to develop our KC area contacts, continue to exploit the Arizona & California markets, and cultivate our new Ohio market.

- We must try to leverage our alumni contacts throughout the country, educating them on what level of player is now required to play for the Ravens.

- We must eliminate walk-ons and project players.

- I must try to convince the administration to alter the travel reimbursement policy so that we don't lose potential recruits due to their not being able to make a visit to campus because of financial reasons.

B. Player Development

- We must re-commit our current roster to spending the required time in the weight room to gain strength and quickness.

- We must push our players to continue to work on specific individual areas of improvement, especially developing 3-point shooting capabilities.

- We must push our players to excel in the classroom. (Continue the 3 nights/week study halls.)

- We must continue to provide spiritual leadership so that each player has an internal compass to guide their decision making.

C. Coach Development

- Continue to use video tapes (instead of costly seminars) of successful coaches to expand and refine my knowledge of the fundamentals and intricacies of successful basketball teams.

- Arrange to have a one-on-one session with Bill Self to talk about how to recruit the best players, how to motivate a player to excel, and what to work on most in practices to maximize those things that most lead to success on the court.

- Continue to discuss with colleagues different coaching philosophies, strategies, etc.

D. <u>Facilities</u>

- Lobby to gain the required storage space in Nolan Gym so that we can run an organized program.

- Move into the new basketball suite as soon as possible so that we can leverage it for this year's recruiting process.

- Refurbish the locker room and make it a first-class facility. This will impress recruits and make current players proud of their "home".

E. <u>Scholarships</u>

- Try to convince the administration to eliminate the tuition discount because it artificially hinders our recruiting and coaching success.

- Be thorough in deciding who receives what level of scholarship.

- Limit the squad size, thus leveraging the scholarship money on more talented players.

F. <u>Budget</u>

- Lobby to convince the administration to increase budgets so that we don't have to spend a lot of time fund raising just to make ends meet.

- Fund raise for special projects, e.g., new basketball suite.

G. <u>Game Atmosphere</u>

- Attempt to get a band at each home game, either by lobbying for the BC band to play, or by inviting the local high school bands to come play on "high school night". (For example, ACCHS night, where the kids get in free with an adult, we honor the two basketball teams, and the high school band plays.)

- Require each player to be a member of a club that has no athletic affiliation. This should forge new friendships, and hopefully attract more non-athletes to come to the games to support their "club buddy".

- Lobby to get a campus-wide coordinated schedule in place so that no other functions are going on during the nights the men's and/or the women's teams are playing at home.

- Work with Steve Johnson to find a way to best publicize the fact that a basketball game is scheduled so that the normal student population is aware of the game.

- Work with the AD to continue to find ways to attract local fans.

Exhibit 12: Twelve Years' Worth of Changes

Physical Changes

Topic	Status as of August 1998	Status as of March 2010	Comments
Basketball Shoes	Players had to buy their own	BBall Program buys shoes for entire team	**1998** – started buying shoes for players
Practice uniforms	Rags	Top of line NIKE practice uniform with player's locker number on it for easy identification	**1998** – started buying new practice uniforms every two years for players
Travel Warm-ups	Unknown	Provide a new warm-up every year	**1998** – new warm-ups yearly for road games
Game Uniforms	A few years old, but not bad. Pants were short, so all players pulled them half-way down their butt.	Top of the line custom made uniforms with logo, numbers, etc. embedded into the fabric	**1999** – started buying new uniforms every third year
Nautilus Equipment	Exercise Room had no weight-lifting equipment in it	2008-09: Nautilus equipment in exercise room moved to old Gym to make room for new Basketball Suite	**2000** -Donors contributed over $10K to purchase "like-new" equipment directly from Nautilus. Put equipment in the room overlooking gym. Konzem later moved equipment to old gym in order to build Basketball Suite.
Nolan Gym Bleachers	No bleachers at either end	2002-03: PIT Bleachers installed	**2002** - Donors contributed about $25K to purchase & install.
Rebounding	None	2002-03: bought	**2002** - Donors provid-

Topic	Status as of August 1998	Status as of March 2010	Comments
Machine		rebounding machine to try to improve hand strength	ed $1K
Gun Shooting Machine	None	2003-04: bought a Gun and shared its usage with WBB. 2009-10: shared cost of a second Gun with WBB.	**2003** - Donors contributed $6K for first Gun **2009** - $3K for second Gun.
3 Scorer's Tables	3 conference room tables with black skirt hung, using Velcro, around each table	2003-04: 3 Professional Lighted Scorer's Tables designed and purchased for use at VB and BB games	**2003** - I asked Danny Zeck (Rusty Eck Ford) and Steve Pickman (MGP) to donate. Got enough $ for 3 tables and put their logos on 2 of them and the Raven logo on the third.
Team Chairs	Multi-colored vinyl chairs from storage room in hallway	2003-04: Raven Logo chairs	**2003** - VB, WBB, and MBB bought 75 chairs for games and locker rooms.
Lighted Backboards	Had one red bulb behind backboard at each end	2005-06: Small red lights outline the backboard as seen in arenas on TV	**2005** - Donor money used to buy these lights
Nolan HAAC Champ Banners (all sports)	Hanging on poles along north wall of Nolan Gym	2005-06: Mounted on walls surrounding court	**2005** - I personally hung them from rafters **2006** – A.D. Konzem had them mounted on walls
National Championships Banners	Mounted on wall in SW corner of Nolan	2005-06: Centered on court & mounted on south wall on each side	**2005** - I personally hung them from rafters **2007** – A.D. Konzem

Topic	Status as of August 1998	Status as of March 2010	Comments
		of Raven Logo	had them mounted on walls
Crucifix	None in Nolan Gym	2006-07: Discovered a beautiful Cross of St. Francis stored in chapel at St. Martin's dorm and placed it on north wall	**2006** - Cross donated by Abbey.
Laundry Room	1 residential washer and dryer placed in Officials' locker room (no vent, so sock was put on dryer exhaust pipe)	2008-09: 3 commercial washers and dryers stuck in alcove in visitors' locker room	**2006** - finally convinced president to put 2 washers & 3 dryers in pre-built laundry room in Nolan. **2009** – new AD moved equipment to visitor's locker room to expand the training room.
Raven Logo	None on walls in Nolan Gym	2007-08: Painted on South Wall between Nat'l Championship banners	**2007** - Coach Folsom and I hired women's bball player Courtney Edmonds and her parents to paint the logo on the wall
Red, Gray & Black Ribbon on walls of Nolan Gym	None	2007-08: painted ribbon around gym to add color	**2007** – Hired Painter to do 3 walls **2010** - Still waiting on Operations Dept. to paint north wall to complete project
Video screens on side walls	Didn't exist	2007-08: Now mounted next to scoreboards	**2007** – SID Pound and VP Mktg Baniwicsz had these installed
Camera	Had regular video camera for filming games	2007-08: bought digital camera	**2007** - Donors contributed $1K

Topic	Status as of August 1998	Status as of March 2010	Comments
Laptop	None	2007-08: bought laptop but was stolen from asst. coach's car 2008-09: bought MAC to be used for film editing	**2007** - Donors contributed $3K for laptops (MAC now dead due to liquid spill – need another laptop)
Nolan main floor	Red and white lined court for VB, BB & tennis	2008-09: Black, Red & White court with huge Raven logo at center court	**2007** – A.D. Konzem spent $30K redoing floor. Design was by-product of VB, WBB & MBB collaborating with A,D..
Controller for Clock	Had two and shared them with softball and baseball	2008-09: bought a new controller so that we had our own	**2008** - Donors contributed $500
Editing Software	None	2008-09: bought custom software that allows editing and easy film review	**2008** - Donors contributed $4K for software license
Travel Sport Jacket	None	Provide fitted sport jacket for every player; seniors keep theirs	**2008** - Donors provide $160 per jacket per player
Transportation	2 15-passenger vans	2008-09: use a leased 24-passenger bus	**2008** - Bus provided by school; Still have to drive bus, but don't have to try to find a second driver
MBB Locker Room	29 metal lockers on carpet designed like bball court	2008-09: 18 state-of-the-art cherry stained wooden stadium lockers surround built in	**2009** - Donors contributed $30K to upgrade locker room in 2009.

Topic	Status as of August 1998	Status as of March 2010	Comments
		white board and 46-inch TV	
Basketball Office	Located in tomb-like room on main floor of Nolan Gym.	2008-09: built Beautiful basketball suite located in former exercise room on second floor overlooking Nolan	**2009** - Former college teammate (Jack Dugan) agreed to donate $50K for BBall Suite to be named after his dad.

Other Significant Changes

Topic	Status as of August 1998	Status as of March 2010	Comments
Holiday Tournament Trips	None	Every 2-3 years take a Christmas trip to home area of one of the players (OH, Chicago, AZ, CA, FL)	**1999** - Donors provide cost of trip (around $8K per trip)
Recruiting Reimbursement	$75 for airfare	2009-10: Full cost of airfare	**2009** - Donors provide $$ for reimbursement amounts
Scholarships	5 for 22 to 24 players	1999-2000: 6 for 22-24 players 2008-09: 7 for 21 players 2009-10: 8 for 17 players	**2010-11**: 9 for as few as 14 players (coach's discretion)
Scholarship Tuition Discount	Total scholarships must average 60% of tuition for each player on roster	2009-10: tuition discount discontinued	**2010** – no discount
Band	Contracted to play every home football game but no basketball games	**2008-09**: AD got them to play at 2 games **2009-10**: AD got them to play at 2	The band did not play at a single game until my 11th year at BC.

Topic	Status as of August 1998	Status as of March 2010	Comments
		games	
Chaplain	None	**2003-04**: asked Fr. Hugh Keefer to be the Basketball Chaplain, which he continued to be through the 2009-10 season	Men's BBall was the only team who had their own Chaplain in the 12 years I was at BC. He was a very positive spiritual influence on our players and a good sounding board.

Other Significant Events

Topic	Status as of August 1998	Status as of March 2010	Comments
Record	**1997-98** under Coach Sick-afoose: 5-26 overall and 0-18 in HAAC **1998-99** under Coach Brickner: 17-17 overall and 9-9 in HAAC; beat 2nd place Evangel in second round of playoffs	**2009-10**: ended year 16-14 and 9-11 in HAAC	**2009-10** - Prior to injuries and illness, was 13-4 and ranked 14th in country in NAIA D1 in late January 12-year record: overall 167-207; HAAC 110-125
Beating No. 1 team in nation	**1950's ???**	**2000-01**: beat 2-time NAIA D1 defending national champ and No. 1 ranked Life University **2007-08**: beat defending NAIA D2 national champion and No. 1 ranked MidAmerica Nazarene University	
20-win season	Last one was **1967-68**	2006-07: **Won 20**	
All-Americans	Last one was Chic Downing in **1971-72**	**2007-08**: Dan Van Dyke, 3rd team NAIA D2 All-American	
NCAA wins	Last time unknown	**2009-10**: Beat Rockhurst and Chadron State, lost in last seconds to	

Topic	Status as of August 1998	Status as of March 2010	Comments
		Wayne State	
Nationally Ranked	**1967-68**	**2006-07**: ranked as high as 10th in country (NAIA D2) **2009-10**: ranked as high as 14th in country (NAIA D1)	

Exhibit 13: Summary of End-of-Chapter Lessons

So, You Want to Be a Coach … Lesson #1:
In order to be available when the "Dream Job" opportunity presents itself, strive to pre-build the foundation required to be a candidate. Also, ensure your spouse understands the sacrifices he/she will have to make being the spouse of a coach, and is willing to make those sacrifices.

So, You Want to Be a Coach … Lesson #2:
If you have a "Dream Job" in mind, get your feet wet early; even if it means doing it for free.

So, You Want to Be a Coach … Lesson #3:
Don't hesitate to ask for help and guidance from experts in the "Dream" field you are pursuing, even if you don't personally know the expert.

So, You Want to Be a Coach … Lesson #4:
Anticipate having to know more than just the fundamentals of your "Dream" field. Widen your vision and be prepared to address key issues that may not be an apparent part of your "Dream Job".

So, You Want to Be a Coach … Lesson #5:
Know that wearing the "Dream Hat" may require you to make it fit sideways, backwards, and upside down.

So, You Want to Be a Coach … Lesson #6:
Working with people is a huge part of coaching. Invest early in honing your people skills.

So, You Want to Be a Coach … Lesson #7A:
Have a plan even before you take the "Dream Job" as to just how far you will go and how much time you will spend developing the "whole person" versus simply developing that person's sport's skill set.

So, You Want to Be a Coach … Lesson #7B:
Know and understand the particular circadian rhythm and the environment of the sport that you will be coaching.

So, You Want to Be a Coach … Lesson #8:
Don't think that since you were a good CEO (or business manager) that you will automatically make a good coach.

So, You Want to Be a Coach ... Lesson #9:

In the coaching profession, getting fired is something that happens often to the good and the bad. Don't take it too seriously; remember when it does happen, take the high road.

So, You Want to Be a Coach ... Lesson #10:

Build relationships as you progress in your tenure; you will cherish them long after that tenure ends.

So, You Want to Be a Coach ... Lesson #11:

Simply strive every day to do your best.

So, You Want to Be a Coach ... Lesson #12:

You only have one life to fulfill your dream – don't waste it.

So, You Want to Be a Coach ... Lesson #13:

You don't have to have the title "Coach" to coach.

Appendix

This section was added after the completion of the book, at the suggestion of my wife, Connie. She thought it would be interesting to post comments from people close to the BC basketball program, especially former players. They were asked to look back on their experience and reflect on what "take-aways" they had from that experience, either positive or negative. These are unedited comments taken from emails sent by these individuals. I hope you enjoy reading them as much as I did, for you always wonder as a coach/teacher if you had any influence on the future of your players/students. Here's what those who responded had to say:

Aaron Hill, 1996 - 2000

"Coach Brickner happened to come to Benedictine half way through my playing career, which can always be a tough transition for any player. I thought Coach Brickner did a good job of trying to make the transition as seamless as possible and worked hard to make a personal connection with each player, much like you would do in the business world during times of leadership change. Many years later, I can more clearly see how some of his business and executive experience were leveraged as a coach during that time. I always admired that he was as much interested in creating a good value system and educational foundation for his players as he was getting wins for the program. Considering most college basketball players at any level aren't going on to the NBA, this seems to me to be the most genuine approach for developing young student athletes for future success. I think Coach brings a unique perspective for anyone considering this field and how to leverage some of the essential skill sets that both the business world and athletic world demand from that position. Whether you decide to coach or work in corporate America, there are certainly some good life lessons and experiences that Coach Brickner can help you with."

Aaron Hill supplement:

[There were} certainly things I really enjoyed and other things I would have done different as an athlete Looking back on it. ...but when your 18-22....you know how that goes. Can't go back and change anything, I just try to teach my kids from my learnings so they can hopefully succeed and limit some mistakes along the way. For example, I wish I would have taken the b-ball In college a little more seriously from a training standpoint and not rely as much on talent or natural skills. ...then again, I went there for football originally, so I was always a little conflicted with what I should really be doing. .....normally all I get is "eye rolls" when I try to give my kids insight and they think goofy dad is preaching again and trying to give them life lessons that they already know. 😊 ....or so they think they know.

Shawn Kelly, 1996-2000

When Coach Brickner made his official announcement that he was retiring from the corporate world to become the head coach of Benedictine College, I was excited yet skeptical. We were coming off an abysmal 5-26 season which included 21 loses in a row so I knew we needed a change. At the same time, I was disappointed that our assistant coach didn't get an opportunity to take over the team because he and I were very close. In fact, another teammate and I had already decided we were transferring with our assistant coach, who was leaving to coach under the man he played for in college. Coach Brickner ended up convincing our assistant coach to stay on as Benedictine's assistant coach, so by default, we stayed at BC.

I have never once regretted how things turned out. I didn't get a full four years under Coach, but in my two years playing for him, I learned more about life than I did from any other coach I had or for that matter any role model in my life up to that point. He taught us the little things, like putting on your socks properly to avoid blisters and wearing proper support for your jock so you would not impair your reproductive capabilities. At the time we laughed about these lessons, thinking they were pointless, but it turns out learning these little things was a valuable lesson for me throughout my life. My progeny thanks Coach that I wore tights, but more importantly, through Coach, I learned it is the accumulation of all the little things that lead to wins on the court, in your career, and in marriage and parenthood. To this day I still make sure I wear proper fitting, snug socks and tights when I exercise or play basketball and I know I have to put in the work to constantly become a better all-around person. I understand that I can't skip the practice and exhausting conditioning sessions and expect to show up at the game and gain glory by hitting the game-winning shot.

While Coach stressed the little things, it's important to convey the impact he had on my life by talking about the big things. He knew playing basketball was not going to be a career for most of us, so he put our education first. Having a coach with a Ph.D. in finance [editor's note: actually it is a doctorate in Management] helped emphasize that he practiced what he preached. His finance class was the most challenging of my college days. Partly because he cut me no slack and the content was difficult, but mainly because I was afraid of disappointing him so I busted my butt to make sure I got an A. Coach believed a great education was the key to a successful career, but he wanted his players to do well not simply to make money. He wanted us to contribute to something greater than ourselves. Coach has a deep belief in something much greater than us as individuals. He didn't push his religious beliefs on us, but he was not shy about sharing his commitment to God. Coach and I couldn't be further apart when it comes to religion, but we share a compassion for living a life of character and believing the importance of living a meaningful life and that has allowed us to maintain a strong relationship throughout the years. 20 years after graduating college, Coach is still a mentor that I reach out to for advice on spirituality, career, family, and fitness.

On one of our recent conversations, Coach told me that as a coach you are never sure of the impact you had on your players. It gives me great honor to be able to share with the world the impact Coach Bricker had on my life as a young man and how he continues to have an influence on how I live my life today. I am grateful to have him in my life.

Danny Young, 2005 - 2009

While I didn't "play" you made me feel part of a community. When I came to BC I didn't have a whole lot of friends or a group to even have lunch with. You gave me a chance because of "theories of coaching basketball" [class]. Who would have thought a drawing of a mediocre sideline inbounds play would lead to me becoming the manager and part of a group of guys who I still remain friends with.

While I believe it is best for the comments in your appendix should be reserved for the guys who played; I just wanted you to know that your love for young people and Benedictine is what I think defines who you are as a coach.

Thanks for giving me a place to fit in and for being a friend.

David Kovarik, 2007-2007

I don't know that I have much to offer other than to say thank you for the opportunity. I left at semester freshmen year '07. My heart wasn't in it and at the time I was struggling as a young man with some personal / family issues. It was the first (and last time) I didn't finish something I started. To this day I regret letting you and my teammates down. You even came to my high school and were part of the signing ceremony. I'm very appreciative for that.

The BC experience taught me valuable lessons:

*finish what you start
"fully commit yourself to what you're doing
*mental health is important
*earn it every day and expect adversity

Fortunately, this experience forced me to grow up and look reality in the face early on. I've missed the game of basketball tremendously since leaving and wish I could have gone out differently. Anything I do in life now, I never want to short change myself or those around me because I know the lasting impact of doing so.

I've had some success in the corporate environment over the last 9 years. Got an MBA a few years ago at night. Have been married for 5 years to my wife Alexandra. We're praying for God to bless us with kids. I think we've even seen you at mass at St. Joe a few times. I draw on my BC experience often ... especially in times of adversity and struggle. When things get difficult, I understand the importance of buckling down and putting in work and having faith.

Thanks for taking a chance on me. I wish I could have shown you who I really am as a person (and athlete at the time). Nonetheless, the experience made me who I am today, and I value it. Take care.

All my best.

Reed McCrory, 1998 - 2002

Coach Brickner's inaugural season was my freshman year, I arrived on campus in August of 1998. I was recruited as a walk-on by the previous regime's assistant coach, Kevin Hackerott, who saw me play in a northeast Kansas high school all-star game circa Feb/March 1998. Thank God he did as I was growing tired of my mom asking me which community college I was going to run track for. 6 foot nothing and 150 lbs. about to play college basketball...at the most expensive school in Kansas with no athletic scholarship.

2 weeks into practice Coach Brickner pulled me aside. I recall him saying, "Reed, you're a good competitor and I'd like you to consider red-shirting to get stronger. If you don't I think you deserve a spot on the varsity roster but I can't promise you a lot of playing time". My response was swift, "Coach I can't afford to be here more than 4 years!" So there I was...on the team with a chance to compete as a freshman.

Two seasons later I felt like a seasoned veteran. I had played meaningful minutes, started more games than not, and had learned of several junior varsity players earning basketball scholarship money while I washed and organized their jocks, socks and jerseys as part of my work study assignment. Near the end of my sophomore year, as finals were wrapping up, I worked up the courage to ask Coach Brickner for a scholarship. He was crisp with his response, almost as though he had rehearsed it. "Reed, if I give you scholarship money now I'd have to take it away from someone else. I just can't do that."

That summer was when I made the most important decision of my life. Stay at BC and contribute to a program that I felt had misappropriated scholarship monies or leave and start anew?

The decision was made. Alternatives were attractive but in the end I wanted to stay. I was raised to not give up regardless of the situation. I swallowed my pride along with boxed Mac and Cheese, Patio burritos and Ramen noodles. Roommates were less than ideal.

2 years later I graduated on time departing the basketball program as co-captain and honorable mention all-conference player. Were there loans that would take 16 years to pay off? Sure. Did I meet my wife after that? Indeed. Were lifelong

friendships cemented in those final years? Yep. Am I still sore I didn't know how close I was to joining the 1,000 point club? Ha!

Yes...that's a lot about me but it's fundamental to properly understanding how and why Coach Brickner remains one of the most transformational figures in my life. He gave me my shot at playing college basketball, strengthened my resolve to fight through adversity, taught me to give back when I can and finally what exactly it means to be a good person. He continues to be an extremely positive figure in my life and has gone above and beyond the call of duty in serving as a reliable reference for me when I've needed it the most.

Thanks Coach! And a huge thanks to Kevin Hackerott for finding my dad after that NE Kansas all-star game...without that none of this happens for me.

Mike Carrington (#34), 2000 – 2004

Coach Joe Brickner.... He brought me to the Midwest. He sold me on Atchison, KS. If you've never been, it smells of a grain alcohol distillery and has a street named Division, that has roots deeply rooted in the development of the town. If that doesn't say enough about his sales tactics, there's always a discussion to be had about the weekend he brought Demario Trent (DePaul guy from Chicago) and I. Coach can sell!

This boy, born and raised in Sunnyslope Arizona, developed over the four years at Benedictine College, in a large part due to Coach Brickner's guidance, both on and off the court. We shared some great moments, some tough losses, and a lot of bad refereeing. Even in the years since graduation and as distance has continued to grow, his quest for health and living a long and healthy life continues to push me to do better as a man. Coach Brickner wasn't your typical NAIA coach. We were taught to play hard, follow the rules, and to attend our 8am classes, even if we got back at 3-4am. I'm glad I got the sleep that morning though, as I was well rested to run my 10, minute-runs. Shout out to Sister Linda there! I got better and developed further with things like this. Coach B also brought in a coaching talent my senior year to help us defend better. We had a special squad that year, with all of the starting five retiring on the all-time scoring list. Four of us were seniors and were robbed in our last game. I've never watched that tape and I don't think I ever will. I'll never forget my time playing for Coach Bricker and the things he did for us young men to succeed then and now. Thank you Coach!

H. Jackson Wood, 2004 - 2006

Thank you for all that you have done for me, Ronnie, and the rest of our fellow Ravens.

I have to say that you were the most "chill" coach that I've ever had. I've since gone into coaching (proud member of the Brickner coaching tree) and I've stolen a few concepts from you. From plays like "Box" all the way down to your trademark Rainbows, the similarities are chilling. I enjoyed the discipline of not cursing and have carried that into my career. When I hear of colleagues getting fired for cursing at the high school level, I can't help but shoot them that classic Brickner grin. I've also been known to holler at a ref the same way you would, "Rick, what did you see?!?"

I'll never forget how I worked my way into the rotation (buying a plane ticket home from Chicago, not knowing that I wasn't originally supposed to go to that tournament). I'll also never forget, later on that year, when I made 7 out of 8 three-pointers in a 20-point loss to Lindenwood. A game or two later, we traveled to Graceland and suffered another 20-point loss. I was confused because I did not get into that game (I thought I still had a hot hand … heck, I always thought I had a hot hand). I went into your office the next day to see if I did something wrong. I asked you why I didn't play the previous night and your answer floored me – you said, "Gee, Jack, I must've forgot!"

All love, Coach, I appreciate you. I will save my haircut at William Jewell in the conference tournament story and my "playboy" Facebook story for your next book. ☺

Dan Raplinger, 1997- 2001

Your first year at BC In 1998 was my sophomore year. Myself and Reed McCrory (year younger than me) were the only eventual 4 year players in the program that were not recruited by you. Ironic or not, neither of those players received a dime of athletic scholarship funds. As the years went on, this was a driving force to push me to get better instead of openly complain and sour my overall positive team experience. Team and family over individual is something you always preached.

208

You were always transparent in what my minor role was my sophomore and junior years and I appreciated that. No BS, just your honest thoughts. I learned from that, you can disagree with your boss, but you better think it through how you are going to deal with it, because it could have potential consequences if handled poorly. I've seen it with players I coached in High School and other employees in the real world.

My senior year started with a fresh attitude that I would be able to contribute in some capacity. That quickly changed when I got a Poochie arm rip that caught my middle finger and broke it. After minor surgery I was out till early January. Coming back with nothing to lose and time running out, there were a couple games where I played substantial minutes and between you and coach Martin decided to start me going forward. We went on a second half conference tear. Beating Top 10 ranked MANC and Evangel at home on Senior night are easily my high points. It was great to share those moments with you as well.

I respected your patience and non-confrontational method of coaching and dealing with the refs. Although as a player, I thought it hurt us in some situations.

I appreciated the opportunity you gave me and how it changed my journey and outlook towards life. Being positive is way better than just complaining about things.

The year I stayed to be a grad assistant, I'm still pissed off you didn't take me on the Arizona trip and took Pete Rose player\coach Jason Bass. But after a previous hotel experience with J-Bass, you probably saved me coach. All love coach.

Sam Hund, 2009 - 2013

"Coach Brickner taught me perseverance in a lot of ways that have extended way past my college years. My only full scholarship offer was from Benedictine, Coach prioritized making me feel a part of the family immediately in my on campus visit and letting me know he wanted me to be a big part of the team. His home visit made a great impression on me and my family, I knew he was going to be the best fit for me as my coach. Although my basketball career was cut short due to an injury, he maintained our personal relationship and encouraged me in my academic and personal endeavors. As a mentor he taught me to think critically and to trust my gut. As a professor he demanded excellence and rewarded diligent work in a similar fashion to his coaching. Although his classes were the most difficult I encountered at BC, I still use the lessons of perseverance and self-worth he taught to this day in my career and personal life.

John Coakley, 2001 - 2005

Wow so much I could say here. First thing that comes to mind are the future professional networking benefits of having been an under-grad asst (glorified manager 😊 in college basketball, especially at a school as well known in the Midwest as BC.

Second is learning from you that it is better to master a few strategies than to try to spread your business approach across the many popular fads and trends of your trade.

Third is that culture and work ethic are more effective than trying to outsmart your competition

Robert "Poochie" Earl, 1998 - 2001

Being Coach Brickner's first recruit was a blessing to me. He treated me as a young man, not a basketball player, which was huge because I'm still living by many things he planted in me. As a player I remember he said get to know your teammates. Find out what it takes to motivate them. Do I need to yell at them or pull them to the side. I use that now as a coach and motivating my players.

I did disagree with certain decisions he made as a coach, which I know he had reasons behind his decisions. As a coach now I understand that more. As a student, he challenged me to focus on my books and plan for the future. He held me accountable on and off the court. The best thing about all this, we still communicate till this day. I still reach out for his advice. He wasn't just a coach but a mentor.

Justin Long, 2004 -2007

One of the biggest takeaways that I received from being part of the Benedictine Men's basketball family under Coach Brickner's tenure was nothing to do with basketball or winning, it was the lessons we learned about being successful in life not just on the basketball court. You don't realize this until many years later because in most cases basketball is all that matters at that point in time in your life. It's more than the game of basketball. It's about being a good teammate, treating others with respect, being on time, learning how to work hard and having a good attitude. These are all things coach would teach us and instill in us while we were playing for him. This would make sure we were successful during and after our time at Benedictine. He taught us how to be good fathers, businessmen, family members, and how to win at life and I thank him for that!

Alexander D. Binder, PhD, 2006-2010

I wasn't recruited to play basketball out of high school, but I desperately wanted to play in college. It's really all I had wanted to do. I shopped myself around to small, local schools hoping to catch some interest and was rejected immediately or simply ignored. Coach Brickner knew nothing about me and had never seen me play, but actually took the time to sit down with me to discuss my interest in playing for the team. He graciously listened to my dad talk me up for a while and then gave me a chance to try out for the team the next time I visited campus. I never played better than I did that day. I couldn't miss in the shoot around or the scrimmage and I really wasn't a great shooter in high school. I still had plenty to work on, but coach said I could walk on to the team and that was all I needed to hear. It helped that I was able to get some scholarships for academics and running track, but being able to play basketball brought me to Benedictine.

From day one (and as a walk-on who wasn't really close with any of the guys), I was never made to feel like I didn't belong or wasn't part of the team. I was coached, pushed to get bigger, faster, stronger, and asked to contribute in the little ways I could contribute. I remember one practice where we were running a fast break drill and I didn't sprint as fast as I could, as coach had asked. In my mind I was thinking about maintaining proper spacing to give the point guard room to lead me with a pass, but Coach jumped on me for not doing what he just asked and made the team run for it. Lesson learned! Toward the end of practice, we would dribble-sprint the length of the floor ten times for conditioning and because I ran track and was in better shape than most of my teammates I would volunteer to do the extra sprint in under one minute to spare the other guys from doing another one. I was just a freshman and just a walk-on, but coach applauded my small contribution. I was part of the team. The most fun I ever had playing basketball might have been the practice where I was asked to imitate an all-American point guard as part of the scout team and coach thought I did alright.

By the end of my sophomore year, the writing was on the wall, and I made the tough decision to focus on track and pursue my interest in campus ministry. I would miss basketball and being on the team terribly and I still sometimes regret that decision and how I went about it, but I appreciate Coach's honesty in that moment and his graciousness toward me afterward. It probably took a small act of God to convince Coach Brickner to give me a spot on the team, but I'll forever be grateful to him for the opportunity and sense of belonging he and my coaches and teammates gave me. I hope to coach my sons someday and foster in them and their teammates the same sense that each of them matter to the success of the team no matter how big or small their contribution.

John Peer, 1999 – 2004 (currently Associate Head Coach at Benedictine)

As a former player and current basketball coach, both Coach Brickner and Benedictine College have played important roles in my life. I was a member of Coach's first full recruiting class in 1999 and then given the opportunity to be a full-time assistant for him directly out of college. Working for him gave me perspective on obstacles he was facing and what he was fighting to change within the program and at the school. Many of those things eventually changed after he left, and though he didn't get to reap all of those benefits, he left the Head Coaching job and the program much better than where he found it. And as a current member of the staff at BC, I'm grateful for his contributions.

As a player I found Coach to be very level headed and business-like in his approach with players. For the first few years there was probably so much for him to do organizationally I think it took a while for the younger guys to build a personal connection with him. I have always wondered about the contrast of coming from the corporate world to now dealing with 18-22-year-old kids (26 if you count Poochie!).

Getting injured my junior year and having to medical redshirt my senior season was probably a blessing in disguise for me. I had never thought about Coaching until sitting on the sideline every game and observing the game from a different perspective. Coach allowed me a small level of input and to sit in on Coaches meetings while still seeing and hearing things through a player's mindset. When I got back to playing the following year, I think this allowed more open lines of communication and allowed us to overcome some early adversity and go on to have a pretty special season. From what I can find I don't believe any program has ever graduated four different 1,000 point scorers in the same year.

When Coach hired me as his assistant, he allowed me a lot of freedom to coach while probably sheltering me from a lot of the everyday politics of the job. He gave me sections of practice to run, directed me where to recruit, and handed over the reins of the Junior Varsity program. Handling that JV program gave me a chance to learn how to connect and build relationships with players, especially in those vital early semesters of them finding their fit in college. I'm fortunate to still be really close with a lot of those guys and have built on that experience when dealing with incoming players to this day.

I was also lucky to have Coach fight for me to keep my job when he left his coaching role at Benedictine. Coach Brickner has always been a teacher at heart. Over the years he has taught me many things I should do and some things I should do differently. However, his main lesson that has stayed with me has been loyalty. Whether you agreed with him on everything or not, few of his players or students over the years would argue that anyone cared more about their Alma Mater and their success than he did.

Scott McEvoy, 2004 - 2008

I want to thank you for giving me the opportunity to continue my basketball career and, most importantly, getting me to BC. Going into my senior year of high school, I wasn't aware of this small school (smaller than my high school) in Atchison, KS. After I finished my senior season of basketball, I felt like had more and wanted to continue to improve and play. I still remember filling out your online recruiting questionnaire and submitting film. After a visit to the campus and scrimmaging the team, you believed in me and gave me this opportunity to continue to play.

Although my basketball career didn't end the way I planned, as I lost the desire and fire to continue mid-way through my senior season, you allowed me to continue to be part of the program. I still brag that I'm the only person to win a JV HAAC championship as both a player and a coach, whether it's true or not :)

Without you allowing me to play basketball at BC, I would not have made a lifelong group of close friends and I would not have met my wife.

Jason Bass, 2000 - 2002

When I think back to my time at Benedictine, and specifically my basketball experiences, I'm reminded of so many positive and influential memories that certainly helped shape who I am today. Coach Brickner was a central figure in my life back then and I'm blessed to have had him lead me and demonstrate what true leadership looked like.

Coach was a player (and still is based on a few recent videos I've seen on Facebook), and could back up any instruction he provided to the team on the court. I have strong memories playing 2-on-2 or 3-on-3 with and against Coach after practice and during the off-season. He was a dominant force when it came to the pick-and-roll - a constant frenzy of energy and stamina that outmatched most of the late teens and early 20-somethings trying to keep up with him.

I remember joining him for a road trip in his 1983 Mercedes after our season had ended to watch some of the national championship tournament at the College of the Ozarks in southwest Missouri - about a four hour drive from the KC metro. On our way back, Coach and I found ourselves navigating a horrible snow storm on narrow winding two-lane highways. In white-out conditions, neither of us were sure we'd make it back without issue. I'll never forget that drive for obvious reasons, but I also felt like we connected because of it.

Today, as a parent and coach for my two son's basketball and baseball teams, I try to draw on several attributes I learned of Coach from our time together at BC.

He is a gentle and caring human first, with a fierce competitive spirit. I appreciated his drive and how he was faithfully committed to his philosophy, always prepared with a plan, but knew exactly when improvisation was necessary to carry out the objective.

I'm more than grateful for the short three years I was able to call Joe Brickner my coach. And equally blessed for the lasting impression he's made on my life as a result.

Chris Corless, 2006-2010

I was not the typical BC basketball player which allowed me to have a much different perspective on what it was like to be part of the program. Coach Brickner gave me an opportunity and that is exactly how I treated it, an opportunity. I was thankful every day that I was part of the team. I also understood my role on the team. I was not the star player but more of a practice/bench player. My goal was to make other players better and more prepared for each game. I took pride in leading the scout team each week and being the best cheerleader I could be on game day. I have taken these lessons and have been able to apply them to my life today. I am thankful for the opportunities given to me and I strive to make the best of each opportunity that comes my way. Sometimes my role at work, in the home or in the community is not to be the star but more of a role that assists in making others better and I attribute my college basketball experience under Coach Brickner to those qualities.

Matt Muller, PhD, 2002 - 2006

Basketball was the most important thing in my life when I came to Benedictine College in the fall of 2002. Being a basketball player was, to me, my primary identity. It gave my life purpose and guided my decision making. However, I'm not sure I've met anyone who loves basketball as much as Coach Brickner. I still remember our first workouts as a freshman when Coach would scrimmage with us. If we weren't ready to play hard, he would make you pay. I remember being challenged by his work ethic and his willingness to sacrifice to achieve his goals. I thought I was a hard worker, but he inspired me to make a deeper commitment to improving as a player. I can still hear him imploring us to give up fun and comfort in order to be the best that we could be. Over four years, though we didn't have the success we wanted, these lessons were engrained in me. I drew on these experiences as a player 10 years later when I was writing a doctoral dissertation while working a full time job and building a family.

 While Coach challenged us to improve as basketball players, he also challenged us to improve as people. This had the biggest impact on me. Like everyone, I wanted to live a life that had meaning, purpose, and joy. However, by the middle of my sophomore year, I was very dissatisfied with the direction my life was going. On the court, we were having the best season of my 4 years at Benedictine. However, off the court, I was unhappy and wrestling with who I was and what I was going to do with my life. Coach brought a larger perspective to basketball for our team by sharing his Catholic Christian faith with us and allowing our team to experience it on campus through team prayer and mass. He also invited one of the Benedictine monks, Fr. Hugh Keefer, O.S.B., to serve as our team chaplain, and had a large San Damiano crucifix installed in the gym. This meant a lot to me as I was exploring the Catholic faith and the meaning of Jesus Christ for my life. A major turning point in my life came in the middle of my junior year basketball season. I was invited to attend a Catholic conference in Denver, Colorado. I had a deep desire to go, but it would mean that I would have to miss two days of basketball practice. Except for an injury, I had never missed a practice or game in my life, but I felt a deep sense that I need to go to this conference. So I decided to ask Coach if I could miss practice to attend. I was fully expecting a short conversation with a clear "no" at the end. But Coach saw that one's relationship with God must take priority in their life, and, instead of a hard no, I received a very supportive approval. The conference changed my life and set me on a course to serving as a missionary and, later, earning a PhD in theology. Now I am able to teach at my alma mater, and help students discover the meaning and purpose of their life. Through his willingness to let me pursue my faith, Coach helped me to see that following Jesus Christ did not stand in the way of basketball. Rather, it gave being a basketball player (and later in life, a husband, father, professor, and friend) a whole new meaning and reason for being.

LTC Todd C. Hanks, 1995 - 1999 (U.S. Army War College Fellow at the Australian Strategic Policy Institute)

To leave a high-level corporate job and move into a second career as a collegiate level coach, especially having never coached at any level before, that takes guts. It was not only a dream of Coach Brickner but also a way to give back to Benedictine College, because of how the college prepared him for success in corporate America. I remember the confidence, structure and high level of preparedness Coach Brickner displayed from the first day he addressed us as a team. The emphasis he placed on defense and intensity is a foundation for any successful basketball team. I transitioned those key lessons learned from Joe into a 21-year career within the U.S. Army, where discipline and focus are required to pursue our national security interests. Benedictine College maintains an outstanding reputation and is a place to establish initial friendships that translate into long lasting personal and professional relationships. That is precisely what Benedictine College and Coach Joe Brickner did for me.

Vince Brennan, 2004 - 2008

Joe Brickner was a great coach to play for during my time at Benedictine College. Not only did he value the work players put in on the court and in the weight room, but also the effort in class and extracurricular activities. That well-rounded college basketball experience shaped who I am today and Coach Brickner, and his experience as an NAIA National Champion, had a big part in that. Even with his

216

calming demeanor, Coach Brickner wasn't afraid to get in your face after an ill-advised pass or poor shot selection … just the kind of tough leadership an 18-year-old freshman needs.

Hope you are doing well. Exciting news on the book! Hope everything goes smoothly on it from here on out. Below are my comments. Hope we see you soon. Stay safe!

Dan Van Dyke, 2004 - 2008

Playing basketball at Benedictine College was one of the best decisions of my life. I think about those times often. The friendships I made, the games we won and lost, the fun we had. I learned a lot during my career at BC, but something that has stuck out to me was, if you want something you need to work hard and go get it. If you don't, someone else will.

Coach did a good job of identifying good talent and bringing them on board. We had a culture of inclusion where everyone felt welcome and got along great, which is a huge aspect of sports and business. Coach did a good job of instilling confidence in his players and let us play with a free mind. I always appreciated being able to make a mistake and not have to look over my shoulder to see if I was going to the bench. I use that way of teaching today. It's ok to make a mistake, but did you learn from it?

I look back on my experience of basketball at Benedictine and am so thankful for that opportunity. How lucky I was to continue to play basketball and have that experience. I gained confidence in myself that I didn't know I had. I met people from backgrounds that were completely different than mine, and now consider them some of my best friends. While our overall record wasn't the best, we did accomplish things and went to heights the basketball program hadn't been to in decades and Coach deserves a lot of credit for that. The things I learned about myself and about teamwork I continue to use in my everyday life as an employee, husband, and a father. There is no doubt that basketball at Benedictine for Coach changed me in a positive way.

-

Julius Staten, 2004 - 2007

Power in faith & opportunity. I was lucky enough to join the BC program in '03 as a walk on. Coach B might tell you differently, but that's what I was. Unlike most, my path to BC was not to be an athlete but to reset where my life was headed. He offered me a role to be near the team after realizing he did not remember me from my visit in the spring. We didn't talk much that year, but I listened to him use his platform with us to talk about faith / personal health. Did so in blind faith.

I was able to learn how to create my own happiness through my admiration of what I perceived as Coach B's freedom. To transition from corporate to education, managing leaders to creating leaders out of young men -- could not fathom the interest in the move. But what I saw day to day was a man who was active, in a loving relationship and happy. Seemed doable, so I strived for those things. Never ask for clarification or even questions regarding "Why?" I just did it. Sometimes completing the exercise will take you further than you ever imagine. There's was so much more I could've provided to Coach and the team, but my experiences outside of basketball weren't great at BC. Just hope I made him proud by staying the course and making it 'til the end.

Thanks Coach!

Tony Anderson, 2008 - 2012

Thank you to Coach B for the opportunity to play college b-ball when I didn't think it would happen for me. My incredible 5 years at BC led to life-long friendships built over countless hours hooping and having a great college experience.

One of my favorite memories of Coach B involved coach and my former roommate/teammate. I guess Coach was just fed up with this particular players lack of effort/ hustle, so Coach B dropped down on the practice floor and did 75 push-ups straight. [Editor's note: I think it was only 40.] Keep in mind, this was not long after coach had major surgery. I'll never forget that day, not only for coach making my teammate and friend look dumb, but also because 75 push-ups is damn impressive for an old man!!

218

Randy Hodge, 1999 - 2002

Thank you for giving me a chance to play for Benedictine. It came at a time of great transition for me from leaving a Historical Black College & University at Morris Brown College to coming back to play in front of my parents.

Thanks for giving me the opportunity to prove I could academically achieve my goals which initially kept me off the court. Thank you for sticking by me as I struggled in the classroom when I didn't know I had a learning disability.

Lastly thank you for believing in me when I didn't believe in myself at times.

Ronnie Tyson, 2003 - 2008

To say I do not appreciate every single thing you've ever done for me would be far fetched. I wasn't a "normal" recruit, I was asked on many occasions to visit Benedictine before I did by Scott and Alex Brickner, I paid them no mind! I didn't wanna leave sunny California for the Midwest, I was just fine hanging out in San Diego with my friends and playing pick-up ball at Rancho Santa Fe. After agreeing to finally go, it turned out to be one of the best decisions I had ever made, not just as a basketball player but as a human being. Being in the Midwest my first couple months was not pleasant for me at all. First it was colder than heck, and then after going through months of conditioning and practices I got hurt the day before our first game. BAM just like that I was out for the season; depressed, upset, and not having any direction I turned to my family, especially my mom during those times. Everything worked out for the best as I rehabbed and came back to finish up four years as a Benedictine Raven. Although we had ups and downs during the years (the five in five out thing I still do not understand to this day), I am glad I finished and extremely happy I had you as a Coach. I met my wife at Benedictine and now we have two amazing kids and it would not have happened the way it did if I did not make that trip to Atchison, Kansas. Thanks for everything and I hope to be able to grab your book so I can read some of the other interesting things my teammates had to say.

CPSIA information can be obtained
at www.ICGtesting.com
Printed in the USA
LVHW111213181020
669076LV00003B/636